The Forgotten Commandment

Copyright © 2005 Dr. Paul T. Evans
All rights reserved.
ISBN: 1-4196-0637-9
Credit to the New King James Bible for all Bible quotations
Scripture taken from the New King James Version. Copyright © 1982 by Thomas Nelson, Inc. Used by permission. All rights reserved.»

To order additional copies, please contact us.
BookSurge, LLC
www.booksurge.com
1-866-308-6235
orders@booksurge.com

DR. PAUL
T. EVANS

THE FORGOTTEN COMMANDMENT

2005

The Forgotten Commandment

TABLE OF CONTENTS

Acknowledgements	ix
Foreword	xi
Preface	xvii
Introduction	xix

Chapter One
The Biblical Foundation For Loving One Another — 1
Chapter Outline for Preaching or Teaching — 19
Group Study Questions — 20

Chapter Two
Greet One Another with a Holy Kiss — 21
Chapter Outline for Preaching or Teaching — 25
Group Study Questions — 26

Chapter Three
Be Kind to One Another — 27
Chapter Outline for Preaching or Teaching — 46
Group Study Questions — 48

Chapter Four
Receive One Another — 49
Chapter Outline for Preaching or Teaching — 57
Group Study Questions — 58

Chapter Five
Forgiving One Another — 59
Chapter Outline for Preaching or Teaching — 88
Group Study Questions — 91

Chapter Six
Rejoicing and Weeping with One Another — 93
Chapter Outline for Preaching or Teaching — 114
Group Study Questions — 117

Chapter Seven
Protecting One Another — 119
Chapter Outline for Preaching or Teaching — 129
Group Study Questions — 131

Chapter Eight
Bearing One Another's Burdens — 133
Chapter Outline for Preaching or Teaching — 141
Group Study Questions — 142

Conclusion — 143

ACKNOWLEDGEMENTS

In the writing of a book of this nature, there are so many who have made significant contributions along the way. Not only are those who help with specific details like editing, but also those who have encouraged, modeled the principles, and individuals who have through thick and thin, walked out these biblical concepts with me. In light of this, Dr. Evans wants to thank the friends and family through the years that have been more than a friend can be.

Dr. Evans also wants to thank most of all, his beloved wife Brenda in whom he is well pleased for all of the time and effort she put into this book. He is especially grateful for Brenda's undying encouragement to write this book and send it to the world!

FOREWORD

When I first met Paul Evans a little less than a year ago, he had just begun a new church, Grace Christian Fellowship of Brevard. He shared with me his vision of wanting this church to become the "most loving church possible." His foundation focus was centered on John 13:34 that says, "A new commandment I give to you, that you love one another; as I have loved you, that you also love one another."

Week after week I have listened to Paul painstakingly present this to the body of the church and may I add with great results. We are not just a church body; we have become a family that is truly learning how to love one another.

So when Paul said that he was writing a book my ears perked up. I was given the distinct privilege to read the manuscript. I want to go on record to make a very valid point that this book needs to find its way into every church and home throughout our country and all over the globe. It is most definitely a must read for personal application, as well as a magnificent tool for group study. Paul has provided everything that is needed in order to accomplish this. With all that is contained within these pages, rest assured you will need to re-read and re-study the contents in this book continually.

In so many of our churches, the talk of love is well verbalized, however the walk of love is absent. These churches, beacons of light that one time shone so brightly have lost their brightness and are in great need to have their lenses cleaned and polished.

Paul Evans believes in building people and relationships. He has devoted over half of his life to doing so. With the writing of this inspired book, I believe he has rekindled a flame that was almost out and forgotten.

Regardless of whom you are or what your vocation, this book will change your attitude towards what it means to love one another. Romans, 13:8 says, "He who loves his fellowman has fulfilled the law." This book will not only reveal how to but will also challenge you to love one another.

I thank our Lord Jesus Christ for bringing Paul into my life, for he is a true Brother in Christ who I love dearly. I thank the Lord also for giving him this vision and his commitment to be a willing humble servant of the Most High.

Robert L. Mabie

This Book Is Dedicated To Two Special Groups In My Life. First, To The Three Women I Love The Most In The Entire World: My Wife Brenda, My Daughter Freedom, And My First Granddaughter Emma! The Second Group Is The Elders At Grace Christian Fellowship Of Brevard Who Have Walked Beside Me Living Out These Truths For Many Years. It Is Their Example Of Christ's Love That Has Brought Me To This Place In My Life To Share Such Awesome Truth With You!

PREFACE

What a wave of shock and sorrow that covered me when I spoke with Mr. Jones! Years ago, when I first knew him, he was a vibrant, strong gentleman who would do anything for you. Sometimes his sweetness and love for God was overwhelming. But now after many years of suffering with a disease called Alzheimer's, not only could he no longer remember much of anything, his paranoia and fears resulted in a totally different personality.

Unfortunately, this is an all too common story among the elderly in our world. It is one of the greatest tragedies to befall a person today. This particular medical condition causes individuals to lose their memories. Ultimately, everything once familiar and known to them is forever forgotten. Alas, they become a stranger to their own self. We can all experience the sense of forgetfulness from time to time, but to forget the most important matters can be disastrous.

There is a story in the Old Testament (2 Kings 22) of a Jewish scribe who accidentally discovers the Law, which was long forgotten and lost to influencing the culture for too long. Society at that time developed into a godless environment and followed the course of whoever led the people, creating a spiritual vacuum throughout the land. People did whatever seemed right in their own eyes, essentially allowing their selfish desires to pollute the right kind of thinking. The story tells how when the law is discovered and read, the people see how far they are from God's intentions for them. This enlightenment results in serious sorrow in all of the leader's hearts, bringing about a move of genuine repentance and turning back to God!

We are nearly 2000 years past the time when Jesus Christ lived and died. No other person in history has affected the world like Him. It is believed and proven on numerous occasions throughout history that

Jesus was and is the Messiah, God in the flesh, and now lives as King of kings and Lord of lords! He is not only the Leader of the Christian faith, He is the Master of the universe and one day every knee will bow to Him and confess Him as the Lord of all. This means that His teachings given to us through the power and direction of the Holy Spirit as recorded in the Holy Bible are to be regarded as the final source of authority in all matters of faith and practice.

Unfortunately, the Christian church at large in all of its emphases, activities, and doctrines has lost or forgotten one of the greatest commandments given by our Lord. This commandment has been minimized, overlooked, diluted, misunderstood, misrepresented, and even reinterpreted to mean or fulfill whatever purpose seems right in any leader's mind today. This forgotten commandment is the second greatest commandment given by the Lord Jesus, to love one another (Matthew 22:34-40).

As in the Old Testament story, the time has come for the whole truth and nothing less than the truth to be discovered and understood about what it really means to love one another according to what the scripture clearly teaches. The purpose of this book is twofold. The first purpose is to clearly and accurately expose the scriptural teachings regarding this matter of loving one another. Second, to begin a renewal within the Christian Church, leading genuine believers to begin living out these teachings, which will ultimately bring about a worldwide coming to Jesus Christ and His Church as the hope for mankind!

I know, this is a huge undertaking. But you must remember, it was the love of God that created and redeemed the world. I believe it will be His love loosed in the hearts and minds of His followers that will also renew the Church and draw the world to Him!

INTRODUCTION

In the true story made into a movie, "Cipher In The Snow," a young child steps off the school bus after school one day into the freezing air and snow covered ground. He didn't take but just a few steps when he fell over straight into the snow. The bus driver noticed out of the corner of his eye and at first gave him no attention. After a couple of minutes when most of the other children had departed from the bus, the driver noticed Joey still face down in the snow. He got out of the bus and went over to pick the child up to see what was wrong. The driver was shocked to discover that the child was not breathing. Immediately, emergency help was called for and when medical help arrived, they made the horrible pronouncement that the child was dead.

It actually took officials several days to identify the child and find his parents. No one seemed to know who he was. The cause of death was also quite a mystery. An autopsy was performed along with a complete investigation of the child's life. It was discovered that this particular child had no friends at school or in his home community. He was unknown at school, not liked by all the children who had contact with him, and most shockingly was unloved by his parents. At the end of the investigation, the coroner's official report read, "this child died simply from a lack of love. There is no other known cause of death."

When I first heard of this movie and its truth back in the late 1970's, I must admit, I had a hard time believing the facts of the story, and then in 1987, I went to work for the Florida Department of Child Welfare. I specifically worked in the foster care division. What an eye opening experience that was. I was dumbfounded by what I heard and saw with my own eyes and ears. The ill treatment and abuse of children in our society is a disgusting and shameful commentary on our culture.

The most horrific experience I had was with a child labeled "failure to thrive." The visualization of that child remains deeply impressed in my mind. What was so outstanding was not the fact that the child was so underweight, it was the baby's eyes. I felt like I was staring into a black hole, like I was staring at death itself. The recollection of this image still causes my flesh to rise.

A baby is labeled "failure to thrive" because there is so little contact from other humans, the baby loses the very will to live. Often these children are left for weeks in a crib with little or no touching or nurturing from anyone, child or adult. From time to time a bottle will be given or a diaper changed, but not often or regularly. The child from infancy recognizes no sense of love towards it and without feeling any love, the child has no reason to live. Loving and being loved are fundamental building blocks of life itself.

At this point, I could provide a large list of statistics relating to other kinds of child abuse, child and teen suicide and homicide rates, teen runaways, etc., that would only cause more shock and awe in our hearts. It would probably cause you to put this book down and put it on the top of your least favorite things to read this year. The point in all of this is to express how desperately people need to be loved! The matter of giving and receiving love is a universal need that is ageless. It is also my opinion that the ongoing experience of loving is priceless. It is the most important experience and activity of the human life. Without love there is no reason or purpose to live!

When we turn to the teachings of Jesus Christ and His followers in the Bible, there should be no surprise that the same truth in its importance stands out boldly too. Unfortunately, the accuracy and clear meaning of love and what it truly means to love one another is watered down, or almost lost altogether in the religious community of our world, especially in the United States. There seems to be so many other emphases and religious ideas that church leaders and churches have taken, causing this matter of loving one another to take a back row seat. It is interesting that in the New Testament, we are commanded, or encouraged to love one another over 40 times. The volume of these verses alone should speak loudly of its importance and priority in the Christian life, but there is more.

A request came to Jesus from a serious religious leader concerning the most important commandments to follow. Why was Jesus asked this? In that day and time there was not only the written law but also oral traditions and interpretations of the laws of God. There were so many that it boggled the mind of any person serious about their faith in God. There were also the diverse emphases of various religious leaders who had their own agendas, which were often set apart from God's priorities. This would leave any person and especially any serious disciple quite confused, scratching their head desiring clear direction. It was out of this confusion that the scribe asked Jesus for clarification of what was the most important commandment. Jesus answers giving two commandments, loving God and loving one another. He goes on to declare that everything else important to following God is depended on actively and intentionally fulfilling these two commandments!

His answer continues to stand today as the two most important priorities of the church and the Christian life. When it comes to loving God, the church has done a good job throughout the years declaring, explaining, and providing opportunities to live out that commandment. It is particularly the second one relating to loving one another that the church is in great deficit of. As stated earlier, This commandment has been minimized, overlooked, diluted, misunderstood, misrepresented, and even reinterpreted to mean or fulfill whatever purpose seems right in any leader's mind today.

The spread of secularism and other world religions pose a great challenge to the Christian Church today. When we are able to fulfill these two commandments in meaningful ways, especially the matter of loving one another, there will be no world system or religion that will block the spread of Christianity. It will spread just like it did in the New Testament and other times in history during great periods of revival. May you and I as we experience this book together, commit ourselves to loving God and loving one another with all our heart, mind, soul, and strength!

This book can simply be read or it can be a source of individual or group study. After each chapter, there are a series of study questions that may help stimulate discussion and thought to go beyond the limitations of each chapter. The first chapter is a little longer then the others because it lays the basis and foundation of the book's theme. The following chapters are practical insights that will help you to clearly understand how to put into practice loving one another. May the Lord give you the grace he has given to all those around me to experience the depths and power of what it really means to love one another!

CHAPTER ONE

The Biblical Foundation For Loving One Another

Babies' need touching and nurturing to live, so do adults. An elderly lady once told me that the only place where another human being ever touched her regularly was in church. She indicated it was the most important element of church life for her. I believe she speaks for a multitude of people. Our day of technology is leaving too many people isolated, alone, and lonely. Loneliness is a curse that plagues our culture. People need love and not just any kind of love, we all need the love God commands us to share with one another from the Bible.

The desperate need man has for love is fully understood by God. After all, He is the one who created us. He knows our every need. There is no other scriptural teaching as clear and strongly taught in the Bible as this one. God has commanded us to love one another and He has made it the second priority of the Christian life. When you consider what 1 John 4:20 says, that if you say you love God and do not love one another, then you really don't love God in the first place. This leads me to boldly state that loving one another is as much the first priority as loving God is. In fact, loving one another is the practical way to demonstrate your love for God! There are so many scriptural passages to examine but for now lets consider the following 4 passages of scripture:

1. Matthew 22:34-40

But when the Pharisees heard that He had silenced the Sadducees, they gathered together. Then one of them a lawyer, asked Him a question, testing Him and saying, "Teacher, which is the great commandment in the law?" Jesus said to him, "You shall love the Lord your God with all your heart, with all your soul, and with all your mind. This is the first and great commandment. And the second is like it, you shall love your neighbor as yourself. On these two commandments hang all the Law and the Prophets."

2. *John 15:12-17*

"This is my commandment that you love one another as I have loved you. Greater love has no one than this, than to lay down one's life for his friends. You are my friends if you do whatever I command you. No longer do I call you servants, for a servant does not know what his master is doing; but I have called you friends, for all things I have heard from my Father I have made known to you. You did not choose Me, but I chose you and appointed you that you should go and bear fruit, and that your fruit should remain, that whatever you ask the Father in My name He may give to you. These things I command you, that you love one another."

3. *1 Corinthians 13:1-8*

Though I speak with the tongues of men and of angels, but have not love, I have become as sounding brass or a clanging cymbal. And though I have the gift of prophecy and understand all mysteries and all knowledge, and though I have all faith, so that I could remove mountains, but have not love, I am nothing. And though I bestow all my goods to feed the poor, and though I give my body to be burned, but have not love, it profits me nothing. Love suffers long and is kind; love does not envy; love does not parade itself, is not puffed up; does not behave rudely, does not seek its own, is not provoked, thinks no evil; does not rejoice in iniquity, but rejoices in the truth; bears all things, believes all things, hopes all things, endures all things. Love never fails.

4. *1 Peter 4:8*

And above all things have fervent love for one another, for "love will cover a multitude of sins."

THE FORGOTTEN COMMANDMENT

Loving Relationships are Commanded by God

Lets consider first of all, the importance of these scriptures. What quickly surfaces as you look at these passages is that loving one another is not an option for the Christian. It is mandatory. It is a part of the standard operating procedure of the Christian life! The Lord understands how vitally important this matter is for His followers so He has commanded us to love one another in no uncertain terms. The importance of these scriptures must be taken seriously.

Jesus indicates that all other matters of the Christian life hang on this. It seems clear that to the degree we are able to make application of this command in our life, it's impact on all other matters will follow suit. In other words, when we love others well, other matters will be done well. If we do a poor job at loving others, God will also evaluate our performance in all other areas as poor. As scripture indicates, man looks on the external nature but God examines the heart (1 Samuel 16: 7). We may look good to others, but God is the real judge of our life. His approval is ultimately of greatest concern.

I am reminded of a particular little league baseball team I coached. The season was not one of our best, but one of the last games we played I'll never forget. The opposing team was one of the best in the league and our boys were playing their hearts out. They wanted to win this game more then anything else in the world. The game was one of those cliffhangers all the way to the end.

We were the home team and down by one run in the bottom of the last inning. There were two outs and a man on second base. One of our better hitters was next to bat and we were all biting our nails to the bone. One strike and two balls were thrown. The sweat began to drip off my brow. The next pitch was a fastball, right down the "pike." I can still hear the crack of the bat as the ball went way out into center field past the centerfielder. Not only could this boy hit, he could run like the wind. It seemed like he was turning third base before the outfielder even threw the ball. By the time the ball reached the infield, both runners were safely across home plate. The celebration began. Yelling and screaming would only put it mildly as to our reactions. But while we were rejoicing on the sidelines, there was a brief conference on the field between the umpires and the other team's coach. All of a sudden, the baseball was thrown by one of the infielders to the first baseman. As the ball reached his glove, the umpire yelled loudly, "the batter's out!"

What! I can't believe this. I asked, what do you mean, "the batter's out?" The umpire informed me that the batter missed touching the first base bag in his hurry to get around the field. This meant that only a simple throw to the bag by the defensive team would cause the batter to be out and both runs would not count, the game was over, we lost. What a tragedy for us. We thought we won the game. But simply because first base was not touched, all the effort in the world could not change the outcome.

When it comes to loving one another, the same thing is true. We can perform in extraordinary ways, healing the sick, moving mountains with great faith, build huge congregations and build huge impressive buildings, even give our selves sacrificially to the point of death. But if we don't have love, then we've missed first base, we have lost! We must never lose sight of the tremendous importance of these passages and their message to love one another. This must be our first priority, before we can get involved with other matters.

The second matter to consider from these scriptures is potential. The weight of this commandment seems to indicate that loving one another is for a good reason. God has not just arbitrarily established this directive for us to follow. There must be a divine purpose working for mutual benefit. Actually, God is always looking out for our best interest in all things. So we need to consider the potential for great blessing found in following this commandment. The question then arises, "what is that potential?" Now, read carefully because what you are about to discover will provide the potential for the greatest sense of fulfillment you can have in your life! Wow!

Everyone knows how things and possessions do not bring happiness or satisfaction. Although jokes are made about having plenty of money being a help to happiness, we all know deep down inside that is not true. But in the continual pursuit of happiness in our country, money seems to be the god too many are reaching for. It is a fantasy to think that if we obtain enough of it we might really get happy. How sad this is because of the truth that everyone intuitively knows that money cannot buy happiness. What is it that is driving us inside for happiness and more? What internal motivation is creating such a desire to be satisfied that we constantly press on, seeking?

This internal desire, motivation, and hunger is found in our emotional being. There is an "emotional hole" inside of every human being longing to be filled. What is the most amazing thing about this internal need is that God created us this way. We can discover this understanding by going back to Genesis chapter one and two to the creation of all things.

In these chapters, we find God creating the universe. His methodology was to create certain things on different days. As God finishes creating certain things, the scripture records that this was "good" in the sight of God. In the creation of man, we see some important factors about man. He is sinless and perfect before the Lord. He also has a perfect relationship with God where he walks and talks with God freely and regularly. Thirdly, man is at the top of the food chain having all of the earth in his possession to dominate and control. It is interesting to note, that these three factors are the goals to some extent for every person on the earth. Actually people are pursuing these very things believing true purpose, happiness, fulfillment, and contentment will result.

But what is very important to discover is that in Genesis 2:18, God looks down at this situation of man and says, "this is not good…" Now when God says that something is not good, it is not good! If it wasn't good in that perfect situation and environment, it surely isn't going to provide any meaningful and lasting benefits today!

What God does clearly point out, as the specific problem is that man is alone. It appears that man has everything in his favor, but he is alone and that is what is not good. Now you must understand that God made man with this "aloneness." It was not something that slowly developed in his life. The real purpose God intended for man in the naming of all the animals was for man to make the discovery that there was no creature on the earth that could meet the emotional need, or fill the emotional hole in his soul. God made man with this "hole" and He wanted man to have an awareness of it too. God then makes woman and when the man sees her he excitingly cries out, "this is what I've been looking for!" The verse states, "This is bone of my bone and flesh of my flesh." The emotional need in his life is now filled. Man is now complete.

All through history, man remains the same. Our fallen condition only exacerbates the sense of loneliness and the emotional need inside. As God has provided redemption for our sin problem through the sacrifice of Jesus, He has commanded us to love one another in the Christian faith as the provision for our loneliness problem. The potential for emotional fulfillment rises when active Christian fellowship involves loving and being loved properly. God's command to love one another then actually provides great benefits for our lives. This should give us clear direction what to stop pursuing and what to start pursuing in order to experience the greatest sense of fulfillment in life!

The third matter to consider from these scriptures is the meaning of the word "love" itself. In our culture today, there are various meanings people place on this word love. Too often those meanings fall so short and are shallow compared to what the Bible means by this word. The Greek word found in all of these passages is the word "agape." This is the highest form of love and is often attributed to God. This is the kind of love God has for mankind. There are numerous meanings that could be discussed at this time, but one in particular I would like to mention is the idea of unconditional love.

God's unconditional love is quite different from the human love generated by us. "Agape" love doesn't need anything in return in order to sustain or increase it. This kind of love is not changed or diminished by anything. It is based on how God thinks and feels about us within Himself, period. As we become Christians which means the Holy Spirit is living within us, then He pours out His love (this agape love) through our hearts (Romans 5:5). In other words, the "agape" love of God is in us and can be expressed through us to one another by the help of the Holy Spirit. This is something that non-Christians cannot do. Unfortunately, too many Christians also struggle to love others in this way. But it doesn't have to stay that way! God commands "agape" kind of love towards others and it is possible to express this kind of love. This is the kind of love we are all longing to experience and to express. It is a love that is real and lasting, not based on conditions.

My wife is like others who love jewelry especially diamonds. Over the three decades plus of our marriage, only on a few occasions have I been able to purchase one for her. Of course when I do, it's a real special occasion. One day while shopping at Kmart, I noticed some very large diamond rings at the jewelry counter. Attracted to look, I was amazed how beautiful they were and was shocked at the low price. I realized I was at a discount store to begin with but I never in a million years expected to find such beautiful diamonds at such a low price. The two and three caret diamonds were under $100. That's right, under a hundred bucks! There was no way I was going to pass this bargain up, so I bought one. Boy was I proud of myself and could only imagine the positive response I would get from Brenda. I planned an extra special time to give it to her. When she opened it up and took a good look at it she simply and mildly said, "Oh, thank-you." I just sat there kind of stunned expecting her to scream, shout, or do something wild, but that was it. I was totally confused and asked what is the deal? That's when she gave me the accurate information. It was a cubic zirconium stone not a real diamond. Basically this stone is a man-made artificial imitation of a diamond. It looks like a diamond, shines like a diamond, but it isn't one. Boy, was I fooled! It sure knocked all the wind out of my sails!

The love God commands us to love one another with is to be the real thing, "agape." Not some kind of man-made artificial imitation of love. Not even the kind of love that can only be generated by the human spirit. This love is from His Spirit living within us and is to be real and lasting. This is what the world and other believers are waiting and actually starving for. It has been my experience to see lives transformed when this kind of love is in operation between people. I have even witnessed it transform entire churches! This is why we are commanded by God to do this and He has clearly made it the most important thing we are to do as Christians. Nothing else and I mean nothing else is as important, as Peter states, "above all things love one another fervently…"

A General Biblical Model of Loving One Another to Consider First

It would be a mistake not to give some serious consideration to the model of loving one another Paul provides in 1 Corinthians 13: 1-8. Theologians and teachers often label this chapter as the love chapter of the Bible. The Apostle Paul in his elegant way takes the teachings of Jesus concerning loving one another and fleshes it out in direct ways to clearly understand. It would be worthwhile for many of us to take inventory and evaluate our own relationships in light of his teaching here. I believe Paul outlines a simple general kind of model to consider in loving one another. I call this passage the "ABC's of Love." It is actually a general model of loving one another to seriously consider.

In verses 1-6, Paul indicates that love is more than just activity; it is an attitude of acceptance. These verses spell out numerous activities that are clearly regarded in the Christian world as outstanding spiritual accomplishments. Often individuals who display and/or operate in these activities are considered saints or great men and women of God. Unfortunately, if there is no love involved with these activities, God considers the activities to be totally worthless and of no value at all. This is shocking! But you say, "Isn't love what I do?" No doubt love demonstrates itself through various activities, but love is not the activities. This is where so many have gone astray. It is too easy to substitute activities for love and masquerade ourselves even to the point of complete self-deception, thinking all the while we are showing "love" when in fact we may not be at all. Paul clearly communicates the truth that love is different than activities in this passage. He shows that love is more than what you can do. In fact, he states through using various verbs and adjectives in the verses that all boil down to one concept that demonstrates love, and that is an attitude of acceptance! This is an attitude that is found in the heart. It is generated there and then proceeds out into the external experience of life, but it begins in the heart with this attitude.

This attitude of acceptance displays itself in the following two ways. First, there is an acceptance of people that are different than us. That difference may be the color of their skin, their national origin, their physical or emotional make-up, or just simply the way they live out life in general. Secondly, we are to accept individuals that are unlovely to us. This concept of "unlovely" in itself is nothing but a perception problem. Distortion in thinking processes can occur because of the way we were raised or other negative influences and experiences in life. As the old saying goes, "one man's trash is another man's fortune," so what may be unlovely to one may be beautiful to another. Just because we think someone is unlovely or we don't like someone or their lifestyle is no reason to reject them, but it happens all the time.

So often because people are different or unlovely we assume Jesus doesn't like them anymore than we do. But how wrong is that thinking! God loves everyone equally the same, unconditionally and there is nothing you can do or not do to change that. God wants us to have the same attitude of acceptance and love for all people regardless of who they are or what they do! This attitude of acceptance has to do with the matter of us loving and accepting individuals and allowing God to do whatever changing He wants to do in their lives. After all, there is a whole world of changing God is trying to accomplish in us. We need to be working on the changes God is facilitating in us and just simply love others by first of all learning to accept them right where they are!

The first six verses of 1 Corinthians chapter 13 provide a powerful message that the church has yet to receive and put into practice. We shouldn't stop the wonderful activities we are involved in, but we must be certain that love is in our hearts first. If not, then all of the activities are worthless! Let's make sure we develop a strong attitude of acceptance that affects all of our relationships!

In verse 7, we discover 4 verbs ("bears… believes… hopes… endures…") that are all in the present tense. The present tense in a Greek verb indicates the kind of action we can describe as continual or habitual. They all point to the direction of what we can describe as believing in someone. The major point of this verse seems to say that love is more than just building up someone, it is believing in them.

Believing in someone goes way beyond just trusting him or her in a particular area. The poor self-image that plagues most of the people in the world today causes so many to live under a burden of "feeling not good enough." Often times to get a pat on the back or some other form of appreciation feels good but it doesn't last or have any changing effect on us. This idea of believing in another does! The continual action of these verbs practiced in life towards others can dramatically create the potential for real change. The verb "bear" found here actually means to support someone like walls support a roof. "Hope" carries the meaning of having confident expectation toward another. In other words, you're convinced that in time the best will occur. "Endure" means not to be hindered by difficulties along the way. When you believe people have value, worth, and potential (which everyone does!), and you're willing to "bear, hope, and endure" with them in life, than that is truly believing in someone. This will result in releasing new energy and direction in their lives and that's what people need today, not just a pat on the back.

After two years of my new Christian life and having no Christian experience or up bringing, I found myself unable to sleep one special night. It was three in the morning and I couldn't sleep. My wife Brenda and six-month-old baby Freedom were asleep upstairs. I sat in the near dark room half thinking and praying trying to convince myself I was making the right decision. Just outside my friend's house where we were for the night was a van and a U-haul trailer packed tight ready for the move.

I felt a call to the ministry and to prepare to become a pastor. That call was leading us out of our hometown of Baltimore, Maryland to a little college town in Graceville, Florida, away from all of our family and everything once familiar to us. I quit my job, sold our house, and this was our last night in Maryland, at a friend's house. Both of our parents could not understand and it was difficult for them to support us in the move. Brenda and I both felt it was best to stay with our spiritual parents the last night. But there I was, honestly, full of anxiety and unsure if this was the right decision. I wished I had years of experience of trusting in the Lord and seeing Him do miracles around me but I didn't. I went over and over again in my mind the call I thought was genuine from the Lord, but I was full of doubts sitting in that twilight, and then it happened.

Out of the corner of my eye I saw a shadow coming down the stairwell. It was my friend Leister Graffis, an elderly man who was my spiritual father. For a while, he never spoke a word. He just sat down next to me and placed his hand on my shoulder in a comforting way. He knew the struggle I was facing. We sat there silent for some time and then he spoke. He looked me straight in the eye and said, "Paul, I want you to know that I believe in you." He gave me a brief hug and with no other words or actions got up and left.

It's hard to describe what happened inside my heart, a huge surge of energy, a mighty wave of confidence, faith that could move mountains or bind the devil himself. It's so hard to describe. All I know is that all of the fear and doubt blew away like a kite in a windstorm. No longer was I confused or unclear, no longer was I even a little concerned about the future. I was sure of God's presence and His direction for my life! One man's statement of belief in me resulted in an explosion of my faith in God and His call on my life. I went back to bed, slept like a baby, got up the next morning and we left on the journey that hasn't finished yet!

It is truly amazing what believing in someone can do for them. There are people all around us ready to give up, throw in the towel and quit. All they need is for someone to truly demonstrate love to them by believing in them to make the difference in their life. They need more than just a pat on the back, they need someone to bear, believe, hope, and endure things with them. Someone to genuinely believe in them as a person of worth, value, and potential in order for them to overcome, get started, and/or make a real difference in life!

In the first part of verse 8, we discover the third part of the general model of loving one another to consider. This is such a simple statement yet it contains profound truth, "love never fails." There is no permanent failure or breakage of relationships with "agape" kind of love. The idea emerges out of this to state that love is more than just being concerned about another; love is about being committed to them.

Commitment in culture today misses the Biblical understanding of the word. Commitment for too many people today simply implies togetherness as long as it is mutually beneficial or just beneficial for "me." Selfishness prevails in attitudes and actions of individuals. It almost appears as if people are saying as long as I get something out of this relationship then I'll stay. But if I'm not getting something, then I'm out of here. Commitment that proceeds out of true love as found in this verse is that there is no break or failure, "love never fails."

Now it must be clearly understood that this is not an open door for someone to take advantage of another or to even abuse or intentionally hurt another. Just because someone is committed to us in this nature is not an invitation to misuse the advantage given. In fact, in this kind of environment, mutual love and commitment should be evident and regularly practiced. It becomes a root system for healthy relationships to grow and mature in.

This kind of commitment expresses itself in two most pointed ways. First, there is a commitment to work with and work through matters with others. Drawing close together through loving relationships can easily expose or surface relational problems sooner or later. When those problems do surface, commitment means every attempt will be made to work through them. This kind of love and commitment creates inside an attitude of "I always want the best for you," or "I have your best interest in my heart," so we will work hard at getting through difficult experiences.

Secondly, there is a commitment to care for another, not only to work with and work through matters. Love at this point means, "You can count on me, I won't fail you." Jesus told the famous story of the man who was on his way to Jericho and was robbed, beaten, and left for dead. Two religious men walked by and paid no attention to the injured man. A third man came by who was a Samaritan and stopped, administered first aid to him, and then took him to the nearest city for medical care and paid for everything out of his own pocket! Now that was love, a total commitment to care (Luke 10:25-37).

At the age of about three, my son Samuel contracted viral meningitis. He became incredibly ill and ran a temperature of 106 degrees for 48 hours. Every 30 minutes, Brenda had to place him in a tub of cool water to bring his fever down a few degrees. After about 20 minutes or so, his temperature was back to 106 again. The ritual of bathing would begin again. This literally went on for 48 straight hours. I was in school full time and worked full time to support us, so Brenda took care of him alone. After the second day I could see the weariness in her eyes and I asked, "How can you do this?" She replied, "Because I love him!" It was the deep abiding love inside her heart that led her to such a place of self-sacrifice to care so much for him. It is God's love inside of us that leads us to be more then just concerned for someone, but to be committed to him or her!

These three ideas from 1 Corinthians 13, form the general model of what loving one another is about. We discover clear direction from this passage that sheds considerable light on how to begin to live as a Christian who will follow the Lord's command seriously. Accepting, believing in, and commitment to one another provide a strong backdrop for us to move on into more detailed and deeper understandings of what it really means to love one another!

Basic Dynamics of Loving Relationships

The Bible among other things is a very practical book, in other words, a "how-to book." It is interesting that so many people find it quite hard to even read and understand, much less put it into practice in their lives. I wonder sometimes why. Could it be we would rather just live our lives anyway we please rather than permit the Bible to direct our lifestyle, or could it be we are afraid of failure or just not interested? Whatever the case, its time to break the mold and start living the most important commandment in the Bible, to love one another!

Looking at how the scriptures explain how to love one another, there is a three-fold principle to consider and understand. This principle can be viewed as the dynamics of loving relationships. When these dynamics are released into motion in a Christian's life will help to successfully begin fulfilling this great commandment. What I am trying to say is, this is the way you make it work!

The first dynamic is to embrace God's love personally. This is where loving others begins. We can't begin to love others with the "agape" kind of love until we have first experienced God's love in our own hearts. Loving others without this experience can only reach the heights of human ability. Experiencing and embracing God's kind of love provides a deeper, higher, wider, and greater ability to love like God loves us ("agape")! Listen to what 1John 4:7-11 says:

"Beloved, let us love one another, for love is of God; and everyone who loves is born of God and knows God. He who does not love does not know God, for God is love. In this was the love of God manifested toward us, that God has sent His only begotten Son into the world, that we might live through Him. In this is love, not that we loved God, but that He loved us and sent His Son to be the propitiation for our sins. Beloved, if God so loved us, we also ought to love one another."

What a powerful passage of scripture. The Apostle John is essentially communicating here that loving other people is what flows out of being loved by God and allowing God to fill your life. This is what I mean by embracing God's love personally. We must open the eyes of our heart to truly see what God has done for us and reach out the arms of our soul and embrace God and His work for our very lives. This is what "salvation" is. As God through Jesus Christ is able to gain entrance into our lives and fill us with His presence (the Holy Spirit), we are ready to move on with this matter of loving one another.

The love of God embraced and operating in our lives is like the difference between a regular hand-held screwdriver and a powered driver. The difference is like night and day. Once you've used a power driver, you'll never want to use a hand-held screwdriver again. Embracing God's love empowers you to truly love others like God loves you.

There is an important point to consider here. There was a man on the top of his house trying to survive a flood covering his home. The waters were slowly rising. He was a good Christian and believed that God was going to supernaturally save him from this disaster. On two occasions, some rescue workers came by once by boat and then by helicopter to offer assistance but the man flatly refused, shouting out to them, "My God will deliver me!" The waters finally rose too high and the man drowned. As he stood before God in heaven, he asked God, "Why didn't You deliver me? I was trusting in you." God replied, "I sent a boat and a helicopter, but you were too stubborn to accept my deliverance!"

More then not, God and His love come to us through other people. We need to understand this and be willing to accept God's love through others. Expressions of God's love towards us can be a humbling experience and for too many of us, we have trouble receiving from others. We want to be on the giving side only, but the dynamic of embracing God's love personally means we learn to embrace it regardless of the vessel. We need to see that the source is from the Lord and embrace it and rejoice in it, knowing this is all for our growth and development to love others like God does.

The second dynamic is experiencing God's word directly. Embracing God's love personally in one sense is experiencing God's word, but this point is a little different. The word of God is not just print on a page. The inspiration and illumination of the Holy Spirit makes God's word alive! It is a living book that is intended to be experienced. There are particular verses and/or passages in the Bible that become energized in our hearts from time to time while we are reading or studying. Sometimes it occurs from just reflecting on a verse of scripture. When it comes to the important matter of loving one another, this experiencing the word of God is essential.

Jesus told us in John 15:7 and following, that abiding or remaining in Him had to do with abiding or remaining in His words. He specifically discusses this idea of abiding in Him as related to keeping His commandment, particularly this commandment of loving others. Listen carefully to His words, picking up in verse 9:

"As the Father has loved Me, I have loved you, abide in My love. If you keep My commandments, you will abide in My love, just as I have kept My Father's commandments and abide in His love. These things I have spoken to you, that My

joy may remain in you, and that your joy may be full. This is My commandment, that you love one another as I have loved you."

Now, let's clarify for a moment. Abiding in Jesus (living the Christian life) has to do with direct involvement with His words, especially His commandment to love one another. What we must understand is that this dynamic is reciprocal in action. In other words, we must do or act out God's word as well as allow it to work on us. God's word is not just for memorization or just analysis and meditation, it is for experiencing!

As we experience various verses related to loving one another, our love for God and others will increase. Like pouring gas into a fire, it will be energized again. When we experience the "one another" verses in the Bible in a genuine community of faith, spiritual growth will exponentially occur both personally and in others around us! Loving others will become supernaturally natural in our lives and the importance that Jesus gives this command to us will be our joy and pleasure!

This naturally leads into the third dynamic of the principle of how genuine loving relationships occur. As we first embrace God's love personally and then begin to experience God's word directly, we then start expressing God's love deliberately. This involves both a choice and a plan. It just doesn't start automatically, there is a deliberate choice to love others. This will not be just an accident.

A popular comedian tells the story of his 5-year-old son's dislike for the family cat. Every time the boy walks by the feline, he attempts to kick it. On one occasion after he kicked the poor animal, his father yelled at him saying, "Why did you do that again?" The boy replied, " It was just an 'acodent' (accident)." When it comes to loving one another like God has commanded us to, it won't be by accident, it must be on purpose!

Not only is there choice involved, there is also a plan needed. This is the specific point that is desperately missing in Christian's lives. Good intentions without the proper equipment and know-how will only end up in failure or a mess. We need a plan and it needs to be God's plan.

Growing up in Baltimore did not afford me much experience growing food on a farm. In coming to Florida, I developed a fascination about growing oranges, especially navel oranges. I figured this would be quite easy so I bought a navel orange tree, planted it, and proceeded to wait for some fruit. I didn't need any instructions or such, after all how hard can it be. Just plant it, water it, let it get lots of sunshine and after awhile, lots of fruit. The first couple of years resulted in absolute failure, not one piece of fruit. The next couple of years I tried harder doing everything I could think of and finally, aha, four oranges grew! I could hardly wait till they were ripe for picking and eating. The day finally arrived! I picked those oranges, delicately peeled them and bit into them to discover, uck! They tasted horrible. They were kind of hard, small, and far from tasting sweet. What could I have done wrong, what a miserable farmer I was.

I lowered my pride and obtained some knowledgeable help. A local grove owner gave me all the right information and things to do for the next year. I followed his instructions perfectly and guess what happened? Right, a bumper crop and they were the sweetest navel oranges I ever tasted. What a difference it makes to have the proper information and plan!

For too long, Christians have attempted loving others in whatever they thought was the right way only to leave a trail of broken and wounded people outside of our churches, bleeding to death. All the time holding on to a self-righteous attitude that "we did everything we were supposed to, I just don't understand why these people feel so hurt." It is time to get God's plan and start putting it into action!

The Bible clearly elaborates on what it truly means to love one another through various "one another verses." In fact, there are particularly 7 verses that come off the pages of the New Testament alive and powerful forming what I call, "The 7-Fold Plan of Loving One Another", God's plan for truly successful Christian living. As we are able to understand them and put them into daily and regular practice, our lives will be radically transformed!

Loving one another is not an option but a commandment from God.

In fact, it is the most important commandment for us to fulfill on earth as believers. I believe it is a desire that burns deep inside of everyone of us because of God's presence in us. Our frustrations of failing at this task have caused many of us to shy away from pressing into more of this truth and practice. The time has come for us to diligently commit ourselves to learning and practicing loving one another whatever the cost. We need to set the dynamics in motion by embracing God's love personally, experiencing God's word directly, and begin expressing God's love deliberately. Acknowledging our failure and turning to the Lord for forgiveness and direction would definitely be in order at this time. A humble and contrite heart will be quite acceptable to our God and this is probably a good place to begin as we now pursue with fervency exactly how to love one another!

Chapter Outline for Preaching or Teaching

The Biblical Foundation for Loving One Another

Introduction: The need for touch and nurturing. Consider the following passages: Matthew 22: 34-40; John 15: 12-17; 1Corithians 13: 1-8; 1Peter 4:8.

I. **Loving Relationships are Commanded by God**
    1. The importance of these scriptures
    2. The potential of these scriptures
    3. The meaning of the biblical word "love" itself

II. **A General Biblical Model of Loving One Another**
    1. Love is more than just activity, it is an attitude of acceptance
    2. Love is more than building someone up, it is believing in them
    3. Love is more than just being concerned, it is about being committed to others
       (1) Committed to work with and work through matters
       (2) Committed to care for others

III. **The Basic Dynamics of Loving Relationships**
    1. Embracing God's love personally
    2. Experiencing God's word directly
    3. Expressing God's love deliberately

Conclusion: The 7-fold plan of loving one another is God's plan for Christian living.

Group Study Questions

1. Share an experience of being loved by another Christian. What made it special to you?

2. How has your understanding of what it means to love one another changed since reading this chapter?

3. Which of the 4 scripture passages listed in this chapter spoke the most to you and why?

4. What has been your experience in Christians "loving one another" in churches where you have attended?

5. How would you describe what being committed to loving means to you?

6. Considering 1 Corinthians 13, what seemed most important to you and why?

7. What was the most important thing you learned from this chapter?

CHAPTER TWO

Greet One Another With a Holy Kiss
(1 Corinthians 16:20)

Standing at ground zero in New York where once the two towers stood, a young boy looked up at his father and said, "Dad, how in the world will they rebuild these buildings?" He responded, "I guess they'll start at the beginning son." Something of such magnitude appears to be almost an impossible task when you try to imagine it completed from the start. When it comes to loving one another, this too is a monumental task. The sheer magnitude of the commandment itself in it's importance and potential might seem overwhelming to some, but we are absolutely committed to learning how to love others like God wants us to and are ready to begin the challenge.

This chapter begins a series of chapters that will specifically address the "how to's" of loving one another. Actually, the Bible is quite clear on this subject. God would not command us to such an important lifestyle without providing the necessary information and direction to successfully accomplish the task. What we find in the New Testament teachings are 7 particular "one another verses" that will create the complete picture of how to love one another. There are some that will be obvious and easy to understand. Others will be surprising and challenging. By the end, we will all be tremendously enlightened and ready to love others like we have never loved before. Our lives will be transformed and will be the catalyst for transforming the lives of everyone who will seriously follow God's command with us! So, let's get started!

The first "one another verse" we will examine is found in three places in the writings of Paul, particularly in the ending of his letters as he is making various closing remarks. The specific verse we will look at is in 1 Corinthians 16:20. Paul writes to the Christians in this letter commanding them to "Greet one another with a holy kiss." This verse establishes what I call "The Beginning of Loving One Another." But what does it really mean? Are we to begin kissing everyone now?? That would lead to some real questions and embarrassment for many. How do we translate this into modern life?

We'll start by carefully analyzing the verse and then make some applications. First, consider the "holy kiss." The concept of kissing in that culture was simply an outward sign of affection and greeting. There is some idea of affection coming from the heart that indicates the genuine meaning of this action. The word "holy" in the Greek means to be "set apart" or "other than." This indicates that the affection from the heart that is expressed in this action is to be different than the normal, in other words, it's to have a spiritual context and meaning. We could easily say that this "holy kiss" is a matter of intentional getting to know one another in a spiritual context.

The Greek verb "greet," which is the primary focus, means to "extend or lean towards another." This verb is in the present tense that indicates the habitual or continual nature of the verbal action. In addition, the verb is in the imperative mode, which is the modality of command. Paul is stating that this action is not an option but is a command or requirement. We can see how understanding the meaning of the words and the verbal action of the word "greet" provides a clear picture of how this demonstrates the beginning of how to love one another.

First of all, we need to understand that the purpose of Paul's admonition in this verse is to begin the building of meaningful relationships. The more you know about someone, the more you can love him or her. Getting to know people beyond the surface level is a little difficult these days. It is easy to hide behind all of our busyness and isolation. I do have to state at this point that unless you are growing in your knowledge of someone you can never love him or her. You must know them to love them. This verse is the impetus to get us on the right track, at least to begin the process.

Second in making application of this verse, we are to take the initiative in building relationships. The concept of the word "greet" as stated earlier, is to lean towards or to take the first step. Paul is commanding that we take the initiative in beginning this process. Also, that we are to make this a habit in relating to our Christian brothers and sisters. As the present tense of the verb shows continual action, we are to make this a regular occurrence not just a one-time effort.

There was a couple I was speaking to who had been married for over 20 years. They were having some marital problems and wanted some advice. In discussing the matter with them, the wife indicated that her husband never tells her that he loves her. As she communicated that thought, her husband rudely interrupted and declared, I told her on the night that we married that I loved her!" He continued saying, "If that ever changes, I'll let her know!" Now, we must understand that this "greeting one another with a holy kiss" is an action on our part that is to be a habit not just an occasional action.

In the third place, this verse indicates that this action can be described as moving out of our comfort zone. We all have some reservations about meeting and talking with people who we do not know. It can be down right uncomfortable. Some people are very out-going while others are quite reserved. At whatever level our particular personality is at, we are commanded by Paul to push past that barrier, even though it's difficult. After all, that's why Paul has made this a command and not just a suggestion. If it were optional, only those active social-types would ever do it. But because this is really the beginning of how to love others, we all have to get moving. If we don't, we take the risk of missing so many that need God's love expressed to them and the great blessings God has in store for us by entering into meaningful relationships with others we would not have naturally initiated.

So, where do we go from here? Well, don't start kissing every brother and sister you come into contact with. But let's begin to start reaching out from our hearts attempting to get to know some others around us. A firm handshake or a hug around the neck will suffice, whatever you feel comfortable doing to extend yourself to another, do it. Take someone out to lunch, get their phone number and give them a call to let them know you're thinking about them, or other ideas you may come up with. Whatever the case may be, let's commit ourselves to begin loving others by "greeting one another with a holy kiss!" Remember that Jesus loved you in a way that the Bible says, "While we were yet sinners, Christ died for us." Jesus demonstrated an example for us to follow that He was not afraid or turned off by any person on earth. They are all worthy of His love, so He extended Himself to them, so that He might know them and they would know Him.

Chapter Outline for Preaching or Teaching

Greet One Another With a Holy Kiss (1 Corinthians 16: 20)

Introduction: In every task, you must start at the beginning.

I. Consideration of the Meaning of a "Holy Kiss"

II. Consideration of the Meaning of the word "greet"
    1. The beginning of building meaningful relationships
    2. Taking the initiative in building meaningful relationships
    3. Moving out of our comfort zone

Conclusion: Let's commit to start building meaningful relationships!

Group Study Questions

1. Share an experience of how you felt unaccepted in a new setting or around people you did not know. What did it make you want to do?

2. What makes you feel welcomed and accepted when you're in a new setting or around new people?

3. Share how difficult it is for you to move out of your comfort zone.

4. Define what the "holy kiss" means to you.

5. What do you do to get to know new people?

6. Make a list of several different ideas that as a group you all can make new people feel more welcomed and accepted.

7. What was the most important thing you learned from this chapter?

CHAPTER THREE

Be Kind to One Another (Ephesians 4:32)

It was 6:30 p.m. and I was driving carefully eastward through a difficult storm, and then it happened. The image was breathtaking! The clarity and fullness of the rainbow was so distinct that I cannot remember witnessing one of such nature. The sight of it left me in awe, and than I remembered what a difficult day I had.

Have you ever had one of those days where it seems that whatever can go wrong does? Sure you have. This was one of those days for me, relationships strained, finances short, miscommunications occurring, and expectations not met. Stress is a mild way of describing my feelings. When days like this occur, you sometimes question your ability to make it another day or even if it's worth trying, then the rainbow appears in all its glory! Wow! This is the promise of God never to destroy the earth by water again, the promise that God is with me to watch over and protect. I perceive the rainbow as the image of God's over-arching presence and power to take care of things. Yes! God is in control and He is able to carry us through anything!

It was the perfect arch of that rainbow that remains in my heart and mind. It was as if the Lord was declaring to me that His over-arching attitude toward my life is a matter never to take for granted or forget. When it comes to the concept of loving one another, there is also an over-arching attitude important to remember and keep fresh in our minds. This is the attitude that must prevail and permeate all of our activity and thoughts towards loving one another. You ask, "What is it?" It is being kind to one another! The apostle Paul makes this quite clear in Ephesians 4:32 in such a simple yet profound statement, "and be kind one to another." Lets examine the verse for a little and than make some serious applications for us to consider and commit our lives to.

In this chapter, we will consider five areas to discuss. First, there is the need for kindness; Second, the understanding of kindness; Third, the results of kindness; Fourth, the choice to be kind; and Fifth, the final points of kindness. This element of being kind is absolutely essential in the understanding of what it means to love one another. It truly is the over-arching attitude of love. Without kindness, our "loving" will morph into something of our own making that will result in more "death" than "life" produced in others!

The Need for Kindness

In addressing the basic need for kindness, one only has to consider for a moment the reality of life. It doesn't take long to see in the very world we live the desperate need for kindness at every turn. The abuse of Iraqi prisoners of war revealed not so long ago, the horrific treatment and torture of men, women, and children in the Sudan and in so many other parts of the world that we hear of regularly on the nightly news, just to mention a few. Within the shores of America itself the statistics of domestic violence, child abuse both physically and sexually are devastating. The "normal" abusive treatment of so many people towards each other is astronomical. There is such little kindness demonstrated on a regular basis in this life and world we live in. The question rises in my heart, why?

I am reminded of the story of Joe, the starving painter. Joe had fallen on hard times. He lost his job at the fertilizer plant, his wife had left him, his unemployment had run out, and he was evicted from his apartment. He packed what little he had in a knapsack made a little sign that read, "Will work for food" and set off down the road on foot.

Toward the middle of the day, he came to a farmhouse. He was getting very hungry, and so he knocked on the front door. A woman answered, and Joe explained his situation, and how he could do most anything and how hungry he was. At first the woman wanted no part of Joe, but he persisted. Finally she asked, "Can you paint?"

"Oh yes, ma'am," Joe said, "I sure can paint. I've done a lot of painting. Just let me show you." The woman relented, found a can of paint and a brush and said, "You go around back and paint the porch, and I'll fix you dinner." Happily Joe went to work.

About 40 minutes later, Joe appeared at the front door. "Are you finished so soon?" asked the woman. "Oh yes, ma'am," said Joe, "But I think you ought to know that's not a Porsche, it's a Volvo!"

Oh no! It is all too easy to make mistakes. Getting mixed up seems to be natural for most of us no matter how hard we try. If you're one of those folks who feel like you make very few mistakes it's probably because no one is brave enough around you to tell you the truth about yourself! Yes it is true, we all have a natural tendency to mess-up more then we realize. The reason is because we all have a sinful nature. This means it's natural to sin. Just about the time you thought you were perfect, I come along and pop your bubble. Sorry about that! Unfortunately, we are constantly in a struggle with the sinful nature residing within us. Listen to what the Bible has to say to us about this.

There is none righteous, no not one; There is none who understands; There is none who seeks after God, They have all turned aside; They have together become unprofitable; There is no one who does good, no, not one. Their throat is an open tomb; With their tongues they have practiced deceit, The poison of asps is under their lips, Whose mouth is full of cursing and bitterness. Their feet are swift to shed blood; Destruction and misery are in their ways; And the way of peace they have not known. There is no fear of God before their eyes.

Now we know that whatever the law says, it says to those who are under the law, that every mouth may be stopped, and all the world may become guilty before God. Therefore by the deeds of the law no flesh will be justified in His sight, for by the law is the knowledge of sin… For all have sinned and fall short of the glory of God. Romans 3: 10-20, 23

For we know that the law is spiritual, but I am carnal, sold under sin. For what I am doing, I do not understand. For what I will to do, that I do not practice; but what I hate, that I do. If, then, I do what I will not to do, I agree with the law that it is good. But now, it is no longer I who do it, but sin that dwells in me. For I know that in me (that is, in my flesh) nothing good dwells; for to will is present in me, but how to perform I do not find. For the good that I will to do, I do not do; but the evil that I will not to do, that I practice. Romans 7: 14-19

Essentially what we discover here is there is an inward force or flow that goes against goodness or being kind. Even though we know better and try hard to be kind, it still is not easy. If you're not convinced yet, just let someone cut you off while driving, or jump into your parking space you've been patiently waiting for. Ah! I think you get the picture. We really have a great need for kindness, both to express and experience!

Actually, there are several other reasons why it's so hard to express kindness on a regular basis, three in particular I can think of. One of those is that we have not seen very many (if any at all), good role models. As wonderful as we may want to believe our parents or caretakers were as we were growing up, the truth of the matter is that they all fell short too. Unfortunately, too many children growing up have horrible role models in this area. The problem is that the role models we adopt through life are demonstrated through our lives. Especially when we are under stressful situations, the worst always seems to show. Poor role models exacerbate the need for us to learn how to demonstrate kindness.

Another reason has to do with physical pain and illness. When you are suffering with physical pain, it's a little hard to think about showing kindness. The pain from your body is screaming in your mind for attention and distracts you from expressing kindness to others.

I love to lift weights for bodybuilding, but it can be quite strenuous. Using a partner to spot you with the lifting is very important for protection. But often when I'm lifting, trying to get the last repetition up, my spotter will begin moving his hands towards the bar to assist. I do not want him to touch it if I believe I can lift it. I am not trying to be mean but under the duress of using my last ounce of strength to lift, what comes out of my mouth is a very rough and ugly sounding, "Don't touch it!" Physical pain and illness have the same effect. It's hard to be kind under such stress.

The third reason why it's hard to be kind is because often there is unresolved emotional hurt inside our hearts. This is very similar in respect to physical pain. However, this is far more serious because we are often in denial or unaware of how these unresolved hurts are affecting us. Some people have hidden and covered them up so much they are no longer visible, even to the person themselves. I know individuals who have so detached from their emotional pain they would swear there is nothing there, but it is, and it is affecting them. The bottom line here is that these emotional pains resulting in anger, anxiety, shame, and isolation are distinctly affecting us in ways that make it hard to show kindness to others.

What does all this mean? Loving and showing kindness will not just happen naturally. There needs to be a serious conscious effort on our part to overcome the natural tendency to be unkind. In other words, there is a real need for kindness in our lives!

The Understanding of Kindness

Wow! Since the need for kindness is so great, it is reasonable now to consider what it actually means to be kind and what does kindness look like in action. I'm afraid everybody has their own ideas about this and most of these ideas are misinterpretations of scripture or just misunderstandings altogether, which has resulted in multitudes of wounded Christians in our ranks. At this point, understanding kindness is not up to anyone's creative thoughts and ideas. We must establish clearly from sound scriptural exposition the true nature of being kind to one another.

Let's first of all think for a minute about where kindness comes from. Where do you think the source of kindness is found? Right, the source of kindness is from the heart of God Himself. This is not something God created or an idea God thought of one day, no way! All throughout the Bible, we see page after page, story after story, the wonderful love of God expressed. It is the theme of the whole book. Kindness is in the center of that love expressed as the over-arching attitude God has towards us.

At the first sin and mistake of mankind, God was there seeking for man, covering man's nakedness and shame, and explaining His wonderful plan of redemption for all of mankind (Genesis 3). Throughout the Old Testament some have interpreted God as an angry judge punishing man at every turn. But this is so far from the truth! It doesn't take a scholar or even a serious Bible student to discover God's true outstanding nature as a God of love, showing kindness beyond human understanding. It could take an entire book to write about and discuss the kindness of God demonstrated in the Old Testament, but we will look at just a couple of passages to make the point clear.

There are two in particular that I would like to call to your attention, Psalms chapter 99 and Micah chapter 7. In Psalms 99, it begins by declaring the greatness of God and continues touching on Moses, Aaron, and Samuel who called regularly on the name of the Lord. These three men actually represent the law, the priesthood, and the prophets. In other words, the message found here is quite extensive and very important to all believers. If I have ever heard or experienced unkindness from other Christians using a "biblical" justification, it usually came from the Mosaic Law, priesthood concepts, or prophetical ideas. The writer of this Psalm hits the highest point with a crescendo of truth declaring that one of God's specific names to be known is the "God-Who-Forgives" (verse 8). This is one of the few covenant names given to God in the Old Testament to clearly describe His outstanding and enduring characteristics. If Moses, Aaron, or Samuel knew anything about God, they knew Him as "The God-Who-Forgives," a God who not only shows kindness but who in His very nature of being, is kindness. I can only respond with a big wow!

In Micah chapter 7, we have the prophet writing toward the end of the Old Testament. After all has been said and done regarding God's dealings with the people on the earth and His own chosen people, Micah is finishing his prophecy to express again who God really is. I believe he was trying to keep people on the right track in their understanding of who God is because our relationship to Him and to other people is essentially based on this understanding. As Micah rehearses many of Israel's failures and sins through history including intentional as well as unintentional mistakes, he declares the truth of God's loving character as it has eternally been established and expressed through human history.

Who is a God like You, Pardoning iniquity and passing over the transgressions of the remnant of His heritage?
He does not retain His anger forever, because He delights in mercy.
He will again have compassion on us, and will subdue our iniquities. You will cast all our sins into the depths of the sea. You will give truth to Jacob and mercy to Abraham, which You have sworn to our fathers from days of old. Micah 7: 18-20

Again, wow! Did you catch the message here? God delights in showing mercy, that's kindness. God deals with our sins in such a way that they can never come back to harm us, He will "subdue our iniquities" and "cast all our sins into the depths of the sea." This is all about removal, restoration, and life. And it all flows out of the heart of God demonstrating such kindness towards us.

Now, lets turn to the New Testament. Just about wherever you look in the New Testament, you will find kindness flowing out of the heart of God and His words to us. I think of the cross of Calvary, where kindness was demonstrated in such a gigantic way. Again, we could write a multitude of books on this subject alone but for space sake, lets examine one passage of scripture, which encapsulates and best illustrates this idea of kindness better than any other passage I have found. It is John 8:1-12. Read this passage several times and look at it closely.

Now early in the morning He came again into the temple, and all the people came to Him; and He sat down and taught them. Then the scribes and Pharisees brought to Him a woman caught in the act of adultery. And when they had set her in the midst, they said to Him, "Teacher, this woman was caught in adultery, in the very act. Now Moses, in the law, commanded us that such should be stoned. But what do You say?" This they said, testing Him, that they might have something of which to accuse Him. But Jesus stooped down and wrote on the ground with His finger, as though He did not hear.

So when they continued asking Him, He raised Himself up and said to them, "He who is without sin among you, let him throw a stone at her first." And again He stooped down and wrote on the ground. Then those who heard it, being convicted by their conscience, went out one by one, beginning with the oldest even to the last. And Jesus was left alone, and the woman standing in the midst. When Jesus had raised Himself up and saw no one but the woman, He said to her, "Woman, where are those accusers of yours? Has no one condemned you?" She said, "No one, Lord." And Jesus said to her, "Neither do I condemn you; go and sin no more." Then Jesus spoke to them again, saying, "I am the light of the world. He who follows Me shall not walk in darkness, but have the light of life."

Amen, amen, and amen! What a powerful passage of scripture. I believe anything you would like to know about kindness is found here. Let's think about this passage. Picture the scene with me. Here is this woman, caught in the very act of sin. She was probably snatched right out of the bed with no clothes on, drug down the street publicly, to where Jesus and a whole crowd had gathered. What humiliation she must have felt. What public disgrace and shame must have covered her. But she was guilty and according to the Law of Moses, now worthy of death.

This was the perfect situation the religious leaders were looking for to trap Jesus. These leaders knew Jesus. They understood the kind of man He was and the message He taught. They knew He was a man of great kindness and so this would be a lose-lose situation no matter what decision Jesus makes. But they are completely baffled by Jesus' response and request of them. Instead of focusing on the woman's obvious sin, Jesus draws attention to their sin. Because they were operating out of a basis of "righteousness" from the Law of Moses, Jesus gently leads them down the path of considering their own life from that basis. Jesus boldly states in verse 12 in conclusion that if anyone lives his life and relates to others from that "basis" then they are walking in darkness and produce spiritual death with their activities. So in the story, everyone leaves and Jesus and the woman are left alone.

Now comes the real important part of the scripture. Did the Law of Moses command for this woman to be stoned to death? Yes it did. So to stone her would be the right thing to do, correct? Correct! Was there anyone there in that scene that was without sin? Yes, you're correct,

Jesus. Jesus was and is the only human who ever walked the earth that is sinless. This means that Jesus had the right to stone this woman to death. He could have done this and would not have committed a sin because He would be following the law and again had all the right in the world to do it. You could say that this was the "right" thing to do. But what did Jesus do here? Please, don't miss this, this is so very important! Listen carefully, Jesus chose to **be kind rather than to be right!** That is correct, He actually established the matter of being kind to another as more important than being right.

I'm not saying that it is not important to be right. I am saying that we see clearly demonstrated in this scripture and in fact all through the New Testament that God is more interested in us learning to be kind over being right. It is in the matter of being "right" that I have witnessed the most unkindness and evil expressed through Christian leaders towards others. It is in the name of being right, that more people have been murdered both physically and emotionally throughout history. And unfortunately, this pattern still exists and goes on today. Why? Because Christians lack clear understanding of what loving one another is all about especially the matter of being kind. I believe that I could go on preaching about this one idea forever because I see so little of it in the Christian church. It is really time for a major change to occur, wouldn't you agree?

Well, the point of this discussion is to share that kindness comes from the heart of God. The real source of this comes from God's heart because this describes who God is and what He is about. If we are going to understand kindness at all, we need to grasp this. It almost goes without saying but I hope you can connect the idea that you need to be in touch with God's heart and allowing His Spirit to flow through you in order to demonstrate kindness in this manner.

There is another important matter to give our attention to in order to better understand kindness. This has to do with the meaning of the Greek word itself as well as the way the verb is used. Lets examine the meaning of the word first.

The word used in the Greek for kindness is "Chrestos." This word means "fit for use, useful, good, mild, pleasant, or benevolent." There is the sense that this word is a very positive action taking place for a purpose. We can easily say it has to do with describing a part of what it means to love others. The most interesting feature to notice here is the spelling of the word in the Greek itself. What is fascinating is that the Greek word for Christ is "Christos." The only difference between these two words is simply one vowel. I believe this provides an important clue to what kindness is all about. You can say that kindness is being like Christ, Christ-like. Kindness can best be illustrated and demonstrated by treating others in the same way Jesus did! The popular slogan, "WWJD" or "What would Jesus do," is directly derived from the biblical concept of kindness. So, if you want to know what it means to be kind, treat others like Jesus did.

Considering the action of the Greek verb (present tense) also enriches our understanding. The present tense indicates habitual or continual action. Kindness is not a once in a while activity or when it's convenient. The scripture clearly teaches that kindness is a heart condition as well as a lifestyle. Also indicated from the action of the verb is that this heart condition and lifestyle is progressive in nature. It is actually a developing process of heart and life.

There is the need for continual growth in our understanding as well as our demonstration of kindness. I believe it is God's desire for each of us to establish what we can call a predisposition of the heart regarding kindness. In other words, kindness is so important in all of our dealings with others that it prevails in the way we look at, speak to, act towards, and respond to others in daily living. Kindness becomes a predisposition to our character, a genuine state of mind, heart, and action.

We do need to grasp in our understanding of kindness, that this matter is more than just doing something nice. This is not just humanitarian effort towards others. Often good deeds accomplished for the benefit of others have been mistaken for the evidence of love. You say, "Just wait a minute. Are you stating that doing good things for people isn't demonstrating love?"

Listen carefully, when you truly love others, you will show it in your deeds. But you can perform the deeds (that look exactly the same) and not truly love someone. Listen to what the Apostle Paul says in 1 Corinthians 13: 1-3:

Though I speak with the tongues of men and of angels, but have not love, I have become as sounding brass or a clanging cymbal. And though I have the gift of prophecy and understand all mysteries and all knowledge, and though I have all faith, so that I could remove mountains, but have not love, I am nothing. And though I bestow all my goods to feed the poor, and though I give my body to be burned, but have not love, it profits me nothing.

These are incredibly strong statements about what it does not mean to love someone. We have considered this previously in chapter one so I will not belabor this. What I do want to get across to you is that kindness is more then just doing nice things. It has to be from the heart and often has to do with even the words we speak. In fact, showing kindness through our words can be quite powerful and life giving to others. The Bible tells us that the power of life and death is in the tongue, these are words spoken by us. We used to say as children growing up, "Sticks and stones will break my bones, but words will never hurt me!" How far from the truth this statement is. Throughout my entire career as a minister and a psychologist, I've lost count of the number of people who were destroyed emotionally by the unkind words from others. In contrast, we cannot overlook the power of kind words in expressing our love to one another. So, in understanding kindness, we must see how kindness is a continual development of the heart, expressing itself habitually through our lifestyle in both words and deeds.

The Results of Kindness
Now that we hopefully have a solid understanding of what kindness is and realize the great need for kindness in the world, let's consider what are the outcomes when kindness is demonstrated consistently. There are three basic results to consider. First, it releases the presence of Jesus. Second, it makes everyone including yourself feel good. Third, it is an

investment that will bring a return. Think about the first one with me for a few moments.

The first result of showing kindness is that it releases the presence of Jesus! Wow! How can it do this? I thought the presence of Christ could only be found in a special worship service or something. Wrong! Understanding that kindness is in the heart of God indicates that when kindness as described above is in action, than God is right there in the midst of the action. The Bible tells us that God is love, so where godly-love is expressed, God is there! In one way of thinking about this, showing kindness is expressing Christ-likeness, it is like putting flesh on the heart and Spirit of God, allowing Him to be visible once again to others. As we set aside our own selfish desires that can include being unkind and we exhibit true love through kindness, the presence of our Lord is released to bless others.

The second result of kindness is that it makes everyone including yourself feel good. The Lord knows that with all the poor image and depressive problems people suffer with today, there is some room for people to feel good. The predisposition toward kindness in our heart coupled with intentional acts of kindness towards others demonstrates respect toward people. Also, it communicates value to another person as well as expressing appreciation to them. These kinds of things create a deep sense of positive feelings within a person. When you see what it does for another, you often experience good feelings too. This means everyone benefits. The over-arching attitude of kindness expressing God's love is the best possible scenario for all!

The third and final result of kindness is that it is an investment that will bring a return. Not only is there immediate benefits, but also there are far reaching blessings yet to reap. It is true that not everyone you feel and show kindness to will respond in the same way. Yes, some may resist or just ignore your efforts. But you must see this as a time of planting, a time of sowing. The scriptures indicate in several places that what you regularly sow in other people's lives is what sooner or later returns to you! Galatians 6: 7 describe this principle of sowing and reaping specifically, "Whatever a man sows, that shall he also reap."

Consider with me for a minute, the principle of sowing and reaping. You always reap later than you sow. There is no instant reaping. We only reap instantly in some lives because sowing from others took place prior to us coming along. In that case we really only reap where we haven't sown. But for the most part, the reaping will come later. Another part of this concept of sowing and reaping is that we often reap more than what we sow. The idea of God blessing abundantly what He calls us to do is at work here. This is a principle we should not easily forget. When we are demonstrating kindness it is an investment that will bring future returns!

Do you know where the absolute greatest expression and demonstration of kindness is found in the Bible? If you guessed John 3:16-17, then you're right. John 3:16 is the Bible verse most widely known today. As you look at these two verses, you see clearly what I'm getting at. Everyone has sinned and is deserving of death, eternal death. But God "so loved the world," He was not willing to rightfully condemn us. He chooses to express His love, His kindness to provide forgiveness and eternal life! Praise His Name! **His over-arching attitude of kindness in His love chose to be kind rather than right in His dealings with us!** Now, where does this leave us?

The Choice to be Kind

All of this information is good to know and catalog in our minds and hearts, but it really leaves us with a decision to make. Are we going to choose to be kind or not? There are actually two parts of this choice we need to consider. One is to choose to be kind, to obey God's directive. The other part of the choice is to make it our continual lifestyle.

Looking at the parts of the Greek verb itself, we discover that it is in the imperative mode. This means that the action called for in the verse is a command, not an option. If we are going to live the Christian life, we must obey this command. This is not for negotiation or for you to devise an alternative plan. It is not even for you to decide to whom you will be kind and to whom you will not be kind. There is no selection process for your options. This is a matter that applies to all. Now, you must realize that God never commands us to do things that are not ultimately for our own best interest.

I can illustrate this by a parent commanding their child not to drink Drano. Now you and I know if the child drinks Drano, they will be extremely harmed and possibly die. But the child doesn't know that. In fact, the child may be thinking that all you're trying to do is to keep them from experiencing all there is in life to do and they might be quite resistant to the command. The same could be true about a number of things like drugs, tobacco, etc. The same is true about requiring positive social behavior. God knows how important it is to be kind one to another and the benefits for all concerned, so He has commanded us to do it whether we fully understand it or not. So, we must choose to obey!

In addition, we need to choose to make this matter of kindness a part of our lifestyle and the inclination of our heart. The verb in the present tense speaks of the need to do this. It needs to be a habit in our life not just an occasional occurrence.

The way I push my workout partners at the gym causes them at times to remind me of the need to demonstrate kindness. I want to go on record here stating that I show more kindness than they deserve! Seriously, there is a great need for kindness in our world. I believe most of us are desperate for someone to be kind to us.

There was a time in my life when some serious unkindness was directed towards me. Some people even publicly stated that I was worthless and of no value. It was a devastating time in my life. There were multiple false accusations made about me and coupled with the spirit of jealousy and hatred by some others who listened and believed the lies, wave after wave of unkindness flowed towards my family and me. But, I am so thankful to individuals who understood what it really means to love one another and expressed that love through kindness to me. Their words and actions towards me were, "This is not the way we see it at all, we think and believe you are a person of integrity and we believe you are still a person of worth and great value to God, His kingdom service, and to us!" What an investment they made and you are reaping some of that return as you read, study, and apply this message! So, let's make a decision right now to be kind to one another!

So then, how do we go about showing kindness? Digesting the understanding of kindness is the first step. It is very important to get that part of the message deep in your heart. After that, the rest will be easy. Think of ways to speak and demonstrate kindness to others by encouraging them, believing in them, and supporting them in difficult times. Think of things you really appreciate them for and simply tell them. Make it meaningful and let it come from the heart. Of course, always apply the principle of wanting to be kind more than being right. This will help enormously! Just keep at it and practice everyday with as many people as you can, especially your family. You will soon experience the wonderful benefits and desire to implement more of this in your life. Start being kind one to another!

The Final Points of Kindness

"Now just wait a minute," one man said to me. "With that idea, anyone can do or be anything and I'm supposed to just sit back and ignore sinful activity or lifestyles and pretend like everything's ok?" Well, this question is fundamentally flawed because it assumes that we are the changers of people's lives. Remember, our job is to love and it's God's job to judge and work in people's lives. As we consider the final points of kindness revealed in John 8:1-11, let's think of the importance of balance.

The principle of balance is worthwhile in just about every situation and system. Our society tends to lean in one of two extremes regarding sin. One is to just simply condemn sin. The other is to condone or just overlook it or call it something else to excuse it. An interesting feature I find with many people who readily condemn sin in others is that they are not so quick to do the same to themselves. They usually condone sin in their own life as mistakes, errors, misunderstandings, etc, etc., but they avoid calling it sin. No matter how you examine it, Christians are not to do either. This may be a little shocking at first thought, but consider with me what we learn from Jesus' last words about love expressed in kindness.

Jesus says to the woman caught in adultery in verse 11, "Neither do I condemn you; go and sin no more." In these short words we find powerful truth and insight providing the final points about kindness. There are three points that surface from this statement worthy of thought.

The first point is that kindness does not condemn the sinner; neither does kindness condone the sin. It is quite clear that Jesus tells the woman He doesn't condemn her. He could have, as previously discussed. But He chooses not to (He chooses to be kind rather than right). But He does not overlook the sin either, He says, "go and sin no more." Some might say Jesus is telling her to go and be perfect, but reality and the exegesis of this passage doesn't allow that interpretation. What is He really saying?

In the Greek grammatical context, we find a double negative in the imperative mode (mode of command). This means that you have to interpret it using the concept of "stop what you've been doing." In connection to this the verb "sin" is in the present tense. The present tense indicates the habitual or continual nature of the action, which tends to speak of a process to carry out. In other words, Jesus is telling her to go and stop habitually sinning, change the course of your life and make it count for something more positive and productive. She is not so much to leave His presence and be sinless and perfect, but to leave and get on with the process of making changes and decisions that will be more pleasing to God. He does want her lifestyle to change, but He understands there is a process to go through for significant and lasting change to occur. Ah! If we could only get this insight into our own thick skulls today, what a difference it would make in dealing with people. This is the type of kindness that truly does lead to change!

The second point that surfaces, is that kindness is a part of God's call for genuine repentance. One thing for sure is we all need repentance on a regular basis. Yes, the truth of the matter is we are all sinners by nature. Paul tells us in Romans 3:23, "For all have sinned and fall short of the glory of God." In 1John 1:8, the scripture says, "If we say that we have no sin, we deceive ourselves, and the truth is not in us." We all struggle with our sinful nature called the "flesh." The point of all this is we are all in need of repentance and kindness is what leads us to repentance. Romans 2:4 shares this powerful truth also, "Or do you despise the riches of His goodness, forbearance, and longsuffering, not knowing that the goodness of God leads you to repentance?" The "goodness" in this verse is interchangeable with "kindness."

We must be careful not to overlook or disregard the power of kindness in this context. There are millions of sermons and teachings on repentance: what it means, how to accomplish it, when is the proper timing, and on and on. But we hear very little about how to facilitate repentance or how genuine repentance can begin. In fact, after 28 years in the preaching ministry including 8 years of full-time seminary education and hearing what seems like a billion sermons, I can never remember one sermon or teaching on the kindness of God leading anyone to change or repentance. Maybe I've been asleep and missed them. But on the other hand, I guess everyone else must have been sleeping too because all I ever see or hear from Christians far and wide is "Tell them their sins, tell them they are sinners, condemn, condemn, condemn!" Or "don't tell anyone anything that might make them feel uncomfortable, you're ok, I'm ok, everyone's ok." We must come to the place of realizing the power of God's love expressed through kindness will lead people and ourselves to deeper spiritual places and facilitate repentance in our lives!

So then, what does kindness do to usher in such life changing power? The third point to consider in answering this question is kindness provides a safe environment for us to face our sin and begin turning from it. Look how Jesus does this with the woman in the passage. Before He says a word to her, He deals with the situation around her to create a safe environment. All of the accusers are gone. In fact, the scripture records that everyone is gone except for Jesus and her. This speaks to the idea that all of the dangerous elements are neutralized and no longer pose a threat to her. Now there is the opportunity for the woman to face her sin in the safe place Jesus has created.

When people are condemned for their sin, they naturally put up walls of protection to guard themselves from humiliation and more pain. They become defensive automatically. Often, in their own defense, they strike out with an offense of their own. This can lead to justifying, minimizing, rationalizing of one's own sin, and/or an attack on the other party inflicting wounds and destroying the other person or person's character. Whatever the case may be there are no winners only losers.

Kindness has the opposite effect. There is no need for a defense. Only a need to allow the Lord to do His work of conviction and then for us to help a brother or sister in the Lord find God's grace and mercy for their life. We must remember that this process is up to God in His time not ours. Our purpose is to continue to love one another (showing kindness) and be ready to help when the time is right!

Now, let's think about the story of the prodigal son found in Luke 15:11-31. This is a good illustration of this love principle in action. The boy's father patiently waited for God to begin His work in his son's heart. We see the picture of the father looking for his son's return everyday. On the day the boy returns, the father is running to assist his son in making his full repentance. At the rejoicing celebration party, we see the father protecting the son from his older brother who only wants to condemn his younger brother. The father's kindness is providing that safe environment for the younger son to face and turn away from his sin.

There is a call from God to every one of us to be kind to one another. Kindness is a sweet place for us to face the bitterness sin has left us with. It is a safe environment for us to become vulnerable to really face up to our bad decisions to sin against God and make our lives and probably others miserable. Kindness sheds God's light and love on horrible situations infusing hope for a better tomorrow and the possibility of real life-change occurring. Kindness is that over-arching attitude of God's love that will usher in the Spirit of God and the kingdom of God into people's hearts everywhere. We must never forget how important it is to be kind to one another and to allow it to prevail in all of our loving relationships and dealings in this world. May we truly commit ourselves to be kind above all else because this is a part of what it means to love others. After all, this is what Jesus is up to every day. Let's join Him!

A Practical Suggestion of How To Begin

It's easy to read all of this and say, "Yes, this is wonderful," then put it on the shelf of your mind and allow it to collect dust. Here is one way I have seen this work very effectively in a group setting. Of course you could do this one-on-one also. I'm sure it will be just as effective. In the group, choose one person to be "it" or hold an object like an apple (in my circles, we refer to the apple as the "holy apple"). At this time each person in the group is to share words of kindness with the person holding the apple. Most of what is said contains messages on how much you appreciate that person for various reasons. The person who is "it" is only allowed to say "thank you" or "I love you too," and nothing else. This is an experience in receiving blessings of appreciation from others. Many have a tendency to want to respond back with all kinds of things, but remember, they are prohibited from saying anything in return except for the two mentioned phrases. Try it, this will be an incredible experience for everyone!

Chapter Outline for Preaching or Teaching
(2 Messages)

BE KIND TO ONE ANOTHER (Eph. 4:32)

Introduction: Kindness is not just a warm concept communicated through greeting cards. It is the overarching attitude in a Christian's life in loving one another!

I. **THE NEED FOR KINDNESS**
  1. The reality of life
  2. The sinful nature of mankind
  3. Why it's so hard to be kind

II. **THE UNDERSTANDING OF KINDNESS**
  1. The source of kindness is from the heart of God
  2. The Greek word gives us a clue of kindness being Christ-like, "Chrestos" compared to "Christos"
  3. It is a developing attitude of the heart
  4. We must understand it is more than doing something nice
  5. We often overlook the power of kindness in our words

III. **THE RESULTS OF KINDNESS**
  1. Kindness releases the presence of Jesus
  2. Kindness makes everyone feel good
  3. Kindness is an investment that brings a great return

IV. **The Greatest Expression and Demonstration of Kindness in the Bible is found in John 3:16-17: It is more important to be kind than to be right!**

Con : THE CHOICE TO BE KIND
  1. A choice to be kind
  2. A choice of continual kindness

THE FINAL POINTS OF KINDNESS JOHN 8:1-11

Introduction: The matter of balance is important. Our society tends to lean in one of two extremes in responding to sin.

I. Kindness does not condemn the sinner, neither does kindness condone the sin.

II. Kindness is a part of God's call for genuine repentance.

III. Kindness provides a safe environment for us to face our sin and begin turning from it.

Conclusion: The call of God coming out of kindness is similar to the call Jesus gave to those people in Mark 8:34-38.

Group Study Questions

1. Share an experience in your life when someone showed kindness to you. How did it affect you?

2. How would you describe the need for kindness in the world you live in?

3. Why is it more important to be kind rather than right?

4. How would the world be different if more people demonstrated this kindness regularly?

5. For kindness to be a state of mind in your life, what needs to happen in you?

6. How do you see the connection between kindness and repentance?

7. What is the most important thing you learned from this chapter?

CHAPTER FOUR

Receive One Another (Romans 15:7)

I have blue eyes daddy, where did I get these blue eyes?" This was not the first time I heard this question. In fact it was probably the one-hundredth time! My youngest son, John Paul was about two years old when he made the marvelous discovery he had blue eyes. For some reason, he became fixated on the subject. At times, my wife or I might find him in the bathroom standing on the sink cabinet starring into the mirror just admiring his blue eyes. If he should by chance see one of us looking at him, he would go through his litany of questions and statements about his blue eyes. At first, it was quite amusing, but after awhile the amusement kind of left. The situation became so annoying, that rote answers would just flow out without giving a second thought.

On one occasion, John Paul was discussing the matter with his mother. He said, Mommy, I've got blue eyes don't I?" "Yes son, you have blue eyes," answered Brenda. He said, "Where did I get those blue eyes mommy and where did brother and sister and daddy get their blue eyes from?" Brenda just replied, "Well, Jesus gave them their blue eyes." "But mommy," he continued that day, "But you have green eyes. Where did you get your green eyes?" "Well Jesus gave them to me," Brenda stated. And then JP made an amazing statement, "Gee mommy, how come Jesus doesn't like you?"

It is utterly amazing how such deep spiritual truth and insight can be gained by listening to our children. History and current experience bears out the awful truth to JP's assumption. When people are different than us, there is a strong tendency to ignore and sometimes outright reject them. As mentioned, history all too often has recorded the horrible persecutions and directly expressed hatred towards others in the name of Christ or religion simply because a person or group was different in some way. We may not burn people at the stake or torture them in other grotesque ways today because they are different, but we have other methods of isolating, rejecting, and basically making people just feel unaccepted or not welcomed. I believe that in God's sight this is just as sinful to Him. If we are going to take seriously this matter of loving one another, than we must learn and commit ourselves to begin receiving one another. This "receiving one another" is the basic foundation of "agape" love. It is what the other concepts of loving one another are built upon. Without this foundation firm and in place in our hearts, every "strong wind" or "storm" that comes along will reveal the weaknesses and instability of our attempts of loving others. Every strong building needs a firm foundation. Receiving one another is the firm foundation for loving one another.

Let's look carefully at the verse in Romans 15. In verse 7, Paul clearly states conclusively, "Therefore receive one another, just as Christ also received us, to the glory of God." First of all, consider the main verb found here, "receive." Let's examine the meaning along with the action of the verb.

The meaning of the verb "receive" is quite rich and is interpreted in three ways throughout the New Testament. In each of these three meanings, the full understanding of this word is revealed and provides considerable insight to consider in this context. One way this word is interpreted indicates to "take by the hand in order to lead aside." The idea here is of helping someone out of a troubled or destructive path. "Taking by the hand," indicates a tender but firm personal touch in someone's life to redirect him or her on the path they are on. If you knew someone and could see they were making bad decisions and placing their present and/or future in jeopardy, and you made a sincere effort to get involved personally in their life (taking by the hand) for the purpose of helping, than you would be "receiving" them in one way. Hopefully, you would not be in a frame of mind to bring condemnation to that person. This would not be "receiving" them at all.

Another meaning of this verb "to receive" is to "grant access to the heart in order to build a friendship." This idea goes somewhat deeper than the first concept mentioned. This action actually means you are letting people into your life. Even though there might be numerous differences between you and them, there is an attitude of acceptance on your part to the place where you desire genuine friendship with them. This of course requires time and energy to accomplish and that's what you're willing to do because you want to "receive one another."

Yet another meaning of the word is found in the scriptures that provide a complete picture of what receiving one another looks like. Often this verb is found in the context of ingesting food. The meaning is "to take to oneself as with food." At first, you might question what does this have to do with receiving other people, but consider for a moment what happens to food once it is ingested into the body. Correct, it is digested and then becomes a part of the body, at least the part of food that is good for the body! The concept that arises here is that when you receive another person they become a part of you or more easily understood, they become family! This is the deepest point of understanding what it means to receive others. Yes, we reach out to help others in trouble to get on the right path by investing time and energy into them, but we also go even further by building true friendships and ultimately accepting them as if they were a direct family member (healthy and functional kind of family) where intimacy and family-like relationships are regularly experienced. Wow! What a difference this will make in the life of our churches where such superficiality and rejection seem to be the norm!

Keeping in mind this understanding of the verb, let's now turn our attention to the "action" of the verb. It is important to keep in mind that Greek verbs differ considerably from English verbs as to their action. English verbs primarily only consider the "time" of the action, like present, past, or future. Greek verbs emphasize the "kind" of action more than the time of the action. Now, I realize this sounds like a Greek lesson, but in examining and highlighting the parts of verbiage of this word, our application and life practice of this action will be biblically sound and obviously obedient in assisting us to fulfill Jesus' command to love one another. So then, let's interpret the kind of action found with this verb "receive."

First, the verb is in the present tense. The present tense speaks of the continual or habitual nature of the action. This can also indicate a process in action that continually is in progress. When it comes to receiving others there can be the process of moving through the three meanings explained above resulting in a growth of closeness and acceptance. Also, this matter of receiving one another is not a one-time occurrence or an occasional activity on our parts. If we are going to love one another, then receiving others is an ongoing experience and demonstration of our lifestyle.

Next, this verb is in the middle voice. This is one of the two "one another verses" where we find the main verb in the middle voice. It is actually quite important. There are three "voices" a Greek verb can be in, active, middle, or passive. The active voice means the subject is acting on an object, i.e. "the boy (subject) kicked the ball (the object)." The passive voice indicates the object is acting on the subject, i.e. " The boy was kicked by the ball." The middle voice means the subject is acting on the subject, i.e. "The boy (subject) kicked himself (subject)." This particular middle voice is reciprocal in nature, which indicates there is action also occurring between two individual subjects as well as with themselves.

Now, what does this all mean? This matter of receiving one another means that not only are you receiving other people as indicated earlier, but also and possibly first of all you need to receive yourself! In the counseling field, I have witnessed more times then I can remember, individuals who had such a poor self-image or low opinion of themselves that they could not even accept themselves much less anyone else. Receiving one another in this context strongly admonishes us to accept ourselves first before we begin accepting others. It will actually make the task much easier!

The final point of action of the verb to mention is that it is in the imperative mode. This imperative mode indicates that the action of the verb is commanded. It is not an option. It is a command to follow. The Apostle Paul is telling these folks that receiving one another is not a choice for a believer; it is the standard operating procedure of the Christian life. In other words, you cannot really love others if you're not in the ongoing lifestyle of receiving one another. Again, wow! This is some powerful truth and insight.

At this point, we could make numerous applications from the above ideas but we must consider the rest of the verse itself and allow it to direct the application, keeping in mind the information already discussed. The verse continues with, "As Christ also received us." In other words, the same exact way that Jesus received us, we are in turn to receive others. As we can describe and understand His "way," we then can make specific application for our lifestyles. So, how did Christ receive us?

There are three distinct descriptions we can explain that provide some insight into the way Christ received us. The first idea is described as intentionally. The decision of Jesus Christ to accept us was not an accident or "plan B." Even before the beginning of time, God knew when he created mankind that we would all sin and come short of His perfection. The Lord knew you and I and everyone else would make mistakes, bad decisions, and basically "screw-up" sooner or later, so He devised a plan.

In the book of Genesis, chapter 3, the fall into sin is recorded. In verse 15, God shares insight into His plan as it is recorded that redemption will come through the woman's seed. At the beginning of the problem, God has and shares the solution He has planned. But even before this particular event, the Bible informs us that God's plan of acceptance of man back into fellowship with Him was long established. The Apostle John writing in Revelation 13:8, states that Jesus who is the Lamb of God was "slain from the foundation of the world." Paul writes in Ephesians 1:4 that God "chose us in Him before the foundation of the world...." In other words, before the world was even created, God had thought through the dilemma man would fall into and He intentionally established a solution. A point of significance to note here is that with this understanding of God's redemptive plan of man's acceptance back into relationship with God, it is easy to see how people in the Old Testament were saved by faith just like folks in the New Testament. There is no difference. God's plan to accept man has always been the same, intentional!

A popular comedian tells the story of his son at 5 years of age and how he would always kick the pet cat. The boy was corrected by his parents on many occasions but just continued the behavior. A favorite saying the child would speak after kicking the cat and hearing his father yell out at him was, "It was just an 'acodent' (accident)!" Obviously it was intentional. So is God's choice to receive us.

Following God's commandment to love one another involves this matter of receiving or accepting others. We must be willing to do this intentionally. We must plan in our hearts to establish this concept as the foundation of how we will love others by committing ourselves beforehand to receive others just like Jesus planned to accept us!

The second idea of how Christ received us is described as unconditionally. There are no strings attached, no conditions to meet. Jesus' love and acceptance reaches from the 'uttermost to the gutter most.' What is so amazing to me is that after He receives us, we don't have to meet some standard or measurement in order to maintain that status with Christ. Of course He desires the best for us and provides His Holy Spirit in us to help us through the process of sanctification, but it doesn't matter if we are good, bad, or ugly, His love and acceptance doesn't change towards us! Wow! Praise the Lord! What a wonderful God we have! This is far from some excuse to do whatever I want to. Actually, it is this knowledge that makes me want to bow down and worship Him forever and serve Him with all my heart!

This concept actually considers the underlying worth and value of a person. It is true that we are all sinners by nature and there is no good thing in our flesh. But God sees past all of that through the sacrifice and shed blood of Jesus and He is able to unconditionally forgive us and receive us because Jesus "paid it all."

In the world we live in, performance measures are a reality. They do have their place and are not necessarily bad. The difficulty arises when we transfer this line of thinking to people and establish particular performance measures or standards that they must meet before we truly accept them. I was in a church that taught that people were like manufactured products. They begin as raw materials and it was the purpose of the church to develop them into finished products. If along the way, someone was not meeting the expectations, they would be severely chastised and I even witnessed the pastor tell people to leave simply because they were not meeting his expectations. Fortunately for me, I experienced the same thing, which was God's supernatural intervention on my behalf to deliver me from such an oppressive culture alien to the heart of God.

God does not see us this way at all. Paul tells us "while we were yet sinners, Christ died for us." The Lord's love and acceptance goes beyond our flesh and sinful nature and He sees a precious "diamond" worth dying for. We are all "diamonds." There is value and worth in every human being that should lead us to receive them regardless of who they are or what they are doing. In fact, it is the loving acceptance that God will use to work His purposes in their life. After all, it is God's job to change people and our job to lovingly accept them, right? Right!

The third idea of how I see Christ receiving us is described as purposefully. There is a purpose God has in mind for us. Jesus is not interested in leaving us in our bad situations, sinful habits, and brokenness. He has a better place for us to live in and experience. His acceptance is an open door for us to go through and start growing! God really wants to deliver us from the penalty and power of sin over our lives. He desires for us to be free from the negative influence, control, and domination of the devil and this world's evil systems. Jesus doesn't want us to be stuck in the same place he first found us in. It is His intentional, unconditional, and purposeful loving acceptance that provides the fertile ground for us to grow!

This principle of receiving that leads to wonderful growth and change is a strong biblical principle that can be generalized in every area of thought. The principle simply stated is that receiving brings freedom and release, rejection brings bondage. Just think of the matter of salvation in a person's life. If you receive Christ, you are free. If you reject Christ, you are in bondage. Receiving means freedom, rejection means bondage.

In our choice to love one another, we must learn to receive one another. This is a part of God's plan of how He intends to work in our lives and fulfill His purpose. If we are not willing to do this across the board with folks around us, we can bind up the plans of God for people's lives. What a horrible thought, and we thought we were serving God! Please Lord, help us to leave our patterns of rejection towards others. Help us to fully understand from this teaching what it really means to "receive one another just as Christ also received us, to the glory of God." And may we begin practicing receiving one another regularly as of this very moment!

Practical Suggestions of How To Receive One Another

Ok, what about some suggestions here of how to practice this? I'm so glad you asked! Get with another person or a group and let them share something ugly in their life. It may be a sin habit or something they struggle with often. After they share what it is, express acceptance to them. You can say things like, "I want you to know that knowing this about you doesn't change my opinion of you one bit. I still love and respect you just the same!" or "I know this really troubles you, but I still love you just the way you are!" Or you might say, "This makes no difference in our relationship!" Yet another statement might be, "I accept you sins and all, it doesn't matter at all to me!" You need to express the unconditional acceptance from your heart truly showing the love of God. Remember, it's our job to love and God's job to judge! This always creates the best possible outcomes and clearly demonstrates the love of God in the best possible way! Let's make a definite choice today to begin receiving one another in the same way Jesus accepts us!

Chapter Outline for Preaching or Teaching

RECEIVE ONE ANOTHER (ROMANS 15:7)

Introduction: Accepting those who are different from us can be a real challenge in today's church.

I. **The Understanding of Receiving One Another**

1. The meaning of the Greek verb "receive."
   (1) To take by the hand in order to lead aside
   (2) To grant access to the heart to build a friendship
   (3) To take to oneself as with food

2. The action of the Greek verb "receive."
   (1) Present tense
   (2) Middle voice
   (3) Imperative mode

II. **The Application of the Concept "Receive One Another"**

1. Intentionally
2. Unconditionally
3. Purposefully

Conclusion: Receiving brings freedom and release. Rejection brings bondage. How do you want others to act towards you?

Group Study Questions

1. Share a meaningful experience of being accepted by another.

2. Why do you think people are so quick to judge others?

3. What part of receiving others is the most difficult for you?

4. What does receiving one another unconditionally mean to you?

5. How do you feel about the fact that God has commanded us to receive one another in this way?

6. What is the most important thing you learned from this chapter?

CHAPTER FIVE

Forgiving One Another (Colossians 3:13; Ephesians 4:32)

Wow! It is incredible that we have journeyed this far. Applying what we have discussed already will revolutionize your life. Addressing this particular feature of what it means to love one another will produce extreme emotions and thoughts in your heart and mind. The temptation is to skip this chapter or just read it too quickly. Don't give in to that possibility. No matter how painful or stressful you feel as you go through this chapter, stick in there. I cannot tell you how very important this matter is and how much you need to fully understand forgiving if you're ever going to really love other people like Jesus does. So, buckle your emotional and spiritual seat belt as we dive in together!

Let me ask you a simple question. What is the main ingredient in chocolate chip cookies? Um, you are right, chocolate chips! Let's try another one. What's the main ingredient in peanut butter? You're right; I can't fool you, peanuts! Chocolate chip cookies without chocolate chips are only just cookies. Peanut butter without peanuts is nothing but butter. Removing the main ingredient completely changes an object. It has in some sense, lost it's purpose for being.

When it comes to the matter of loving one another, forgiveness is the main ingredient! Forgiving one another is the center focus of love. Love without forgiveness is something far away from the love of God we find in Jesus. Forgiveness is right in the center of love! Listen to a couple of these quotes from famous people from the past. "To understand everything means to forgive everything," a French proverb. Mark Twain wrote, "Forgiveness is the fragrance the violet sheds on the heel that has crushed it." Mahatma Gandhi said, "The weak can never forgive. Forgiveness is the attribute of the strong." Finally, Francois Duc De La

Rochefoucauld, a French writer in the 1600's recorded, "One forgives to the degree that one loves."

The need for giving and receiving forgiveness is a well-understood fact in our society. In fact, history bears out this need in every civilization known of.

People are somewhat like porcupines in their emotional nature. The sinful nature we all partake of causes us to be sharp around the edges as well as quite sensitive deep inside. Of course there are some that are more than others. The closer we get to one another, the more potential of sticking and hurting one another. This is why so many people feel safe in a distant relationship with others. They have experienced hurt in other relationships and now they live guarded, distant and isolated. There is an old saying that states, "Better to have loved and lost, than to never have loved at all." I believe there are too many individuals that would disagree with that concept. The pain of their hurt is so great that they would rather have never loved in the first place. So in some emotional barricade, they spend their lives separated from real life and the wonder of loving relationships, missing God's great purpose and fulfillment in their lives!

It's time for us to examine our scripture and allow the Holy Spirit to begin to teach us and prepare us for living in a way that forgiving one another is regularly active in our lives.

The Action of Forgiveness Defined

Let's first of all consider defining what it means to forgive. In both scripture verses (Colossians 3:13 and Ephesians 4:32), the Greek word used for the verb "forgive" is "charidzomai." The concept of the action taking place here is the matter of "giving something." The big question is what are we to give? This can best be understood by the root word of "charidzomai," "charis." "Charis" is the Greek word for grace! What we are to give is grace. You ask, "What is grace?" I'm so glad you asked. Grace is defined as the unmerited favor God provides to us. It is a matter of not getting what you do deserve or getting what you haven't earned or deserved.

When we choose to forgive, we are simply giving what someone may not deserve but it is a matter of giving grace. It is so easy and quite natural when someone hurts you to hold him or her in your judgment, a bitter judgment at that. Forgiveness is actually releasing them from your bitter judgment and turning them over to the Lord who is the true and righteous judge. You can really walk away from this kind of experience feeling so relieved.

It is important though for us to consider what forgiveness is not. This can clear up the meaning of what Paul is calling us to do in these verses. There are 8 particular factors to give attention to. We can clearly state that forgiveness is not:

1. **A feeling** - Too many people get caught up in believing they must feel something internally before they can forgive. If there is no feeling involved, there is no forgiveness given. Forgiveness is an act of the will, a choice to make, not a feeling to experience!

2. **A healing** - Just because you have released someone from your bitter judgment in forgiving him or her, does not mean automatically that healing can be experienced in that hurt. Healing really is a separate experience. It is true that emotional healing cannot occur without forgiveness, but understand that forgiveness is only the first step in emotional healing. In other words, you can forgive and still feel hurt and pain associated with the matter. If you do, than you need someone who can help you obtain healing beyond the fact you have chosen to forgive.

3. **Pretending the offence didn't matter** - I have witnessed many people both young and old who refuse to forgive another because they felt like if they chose to forgive than they would have to act or believe the offence meant little or nothing. The truth of the matter is that whatever the offense, if you are wounded and hurt as a result of it, it's a big deal! Forgiving one another doesn't mean it didn't matter, it does. Forgiving means you release them from your bitter judgment even though it hurt deeply.

4. **Approval and permission** – This point has to do with

thinking that if you forgive someone than you are saying to them, "What you did to me is ok, so you can continue." This is so far from the truth. Forgiveness as defined in the Bible is not indicating approval or permission to continue hurting me. What a person did to me really hurt and I don't want it to happen again. If I have to break the relationship or call for help from proper authorities I will. We must deal properly with these kinds of situations. But I can still in my heart release a person from my bitter judgment and not carry around a grudge or deep resentment in my heart. I can be free inside by forgiving but I will not approve of or permit continuation of this negative behavior.

5. **Toleration** – Toleration is similar to approval and permission but differs in the sense that you believe there is nothing you can do about the situation so you just quietly allow it to continue. You say that you forgive but all you are really doing is tolerating the actions of others. This brings a person to the sense of "I'm not forgiving because I'll just have to keep putting up with this stuff." Forgiveness is not toleration. As in the previous point, proper actions need to be taken. Forgiveness is releasing that person from your bitter judgment and turning them over to the Lord to deal with. This is what releases you from the bitterness in your heart so you can have peace and joy in your life. So, forgiveness is not toleration.

6. **Equal with trust** – There have been so many people who confuse forgiveness with trust. Forgiveness biblically speaking is an immediate action that can occur in a split second. Trust on the other hand, may take a lifetime to build. When trust is shattered in a relationship, it will take a long time to rebuild through proper actions and the faithful demonstration of integrity. The point here is that forgiveness is not equal with trust. Anyone who desires our trust too quickly needs a reality check, but desiring forgiveness immediately is a healthy request.

7. **Keeping score** – Unfortunately, some people forgive only for the purpose to have "one up" on another person. They have the attitude of letting someone off the hook to "keep him or

her on a string." They forgive to keep score, to remember for future reference and potential bashing for whatever purpose. This is pure manipulation and devilish in nature. We are called to forgive and let the offense go, to release someone from our bitter judgment and leave them in God's hands to deal with. After all, the Lord is quite capable of appropriately handling matters. By the way, He has considerable experience and expertise in this area. Let's trust Him to deal rightfully with others.

8. **Religious cover-up** – The last point I want to make regarding what forgiveness is not, is this matter of spiritualizing and religiously presenting nothing more than a self-righteous attitude. I have heard, "Forgiving is what I'm supposed to do, so because I'm a Christian, I'll forgive you." I can almost hear in between the lines, "But don't you ever let it happen again or you'll wish you'd never been born!" Internally there is a deep-seated grudge. This is not even close to what forgiveness means or is all about.

Consideration of these elements of what it doesn't mean to forgive assists in helping to further define forgiveness. The final area to discuss in giving definition to this main ingredient of love is to look at the verb's action. The grammatical breakdown of a Greek verb is paramount in clearly understanding it's meaning as discussed in the previous chapter. The insights from the action of this verb "forgive," provide in-depth clarity to its definition. There are three important points of grammar to discuss.

The first grammatical point has to do with the verbal tense. It is in the present tense. As discussed before, the present tense in the Greek indicates continual or habitual action. You can say that this is a way to live or a lifestyle to adopt. Forgiving one another is not just for special occasions or whenever the mood hits us. This activity should be a regular part of our relational interaction with others. As it is the main ingredient of loving one another, forgiving should become like an automatic response to offenses, not something we need others to remind us of or push us into.

The second grammatical point indicates the verb is in the imperative mode. This tells us that this is a command not an option. The Apostle Paul understands how vital forgiving one another is to fulfill the commandment to love one another, so he does not imply that forgiving one another is just a good idea to consider. It is standard equipment and absolutely necessary to live the Christian life successfully! This is not a suggestion, it is a commandment! There should be no debate over who should be forgiven or which matters merit forgiveness. We are to forgive regardless of the offense or how many times the offense occurs. Forgiveness is the only alternative!

The third grammatical feature to examine is the voice of the verb. This particular verb is found in the middle voice. This is quite interesting. Most of the one another verses we will look at in this book are simply in the normal active voice. Only a couple of them are in the middle voice. It is very important to our understanding of this forgiveness to realize this point. Although I shared information about the Greek verbal "voice" previously, I would like to share again because of its importance.

There are three voices in the Greek verb, the active, middle, and passive voice. The active voice indicates that the action of the subject is directed towards the object in the sentence. This is best understood by this example, "**The boy** (subject) **kicked** (verbal action) **the ball** (object)." The passive voice is where the subject is the recipient of the action of the object. Seen like this, "**The boy** (subject) **is kicked** (verbal action) **by the ball** (object)." The middle voice is where the subject acts on himself. Seen like this, "**The boy** (subject) **kicked** (verbal action) **himself** (subject)." In other words, the subject is also the object of the action.

Now let's consider this carefully, we do not want to miss this. Forgiving is in the middle voice. This means that the first point of action to occur is that we must forgive ourselves, even before we begin the process of forgiving others! I have witnessed over and over again how people can receive God's forgiveness, receive forgiveness from others, but when it comes to forgiving themselves of mistakes, failures, etc, etc, they just can't do it or have an incredibly hard time trying. I had one man tell me, "I do believe that God can forgive me for what I've done, but I really don't think I can forgive myself." Unforgiveness towards ourselves is just as dangerous as not forgiving others. In fact, according to what we find here, forgiving self is the first step, a higher priority to forgiving others! Wow!

This is not determined by what you've done or how often you've done it. There is no measurement by which forgiveness is determined feasible. Loving is a matter of loving self as well as others. Forgiveness is about facing the demons of your past, those skeletons in your closet and exposing them to the genuine love of God that resides in your heart and releasing yourself from your own bitter judgment! There is a good chance that the Holy Spirit is calling up some things in your heart that you are holding against yourself. Why don't you just put this book down right this second and make the choice to forgive yourself? Release yourself from your own bitter judgment and allow God's love to flood your heart and mind this very minute!! Be free from the emotional prison of your own making, right now!

Understanding forgiveness is very important if we are going to activate the process in our lives. Forgiveness is about giving grace, unmerited favor and releasing yourself as well as others from our own bitter judgment towards them. Actually, forgiveness has to do more with you and your relationship with God than the other person. It is easy to fall into the trap of only forgiving if the other person asks for forgiveness. Forgiving one another as found in the scripture, as it is in line with the whole concept of loving one another, is about God working His grace of forgiveness in you and then you sharing that same love with others!

The Action of Forgiveness Described

Let's now turn our attention to how the Bible describes forgiveness. Our scripture states that we are to forgive others in the same way that God in Christ forgave us. Considering this idea, there are three areas to think about in describing forgiveness. I see that Jesus chose to do it, He suffered to do it, and He continues to do it.

When I think about what it means to be God, why didn't God just dispose of mankind and start over with a better model? After all, God is timeless and able to see the future as the present. When He considered all of history and all of the horrible sins mankind would commit, it just seems like a better idea just to completely discard the human race. In all of God's acts of kindness and mercy and the thousands of chances He has provided to us, we still continue in sinful practices. The choice seems obvious to me what God should do, but… He had a different idea! He chose to forgive us! This is a choice we should all rejoice about!

What is so interesting about God's choice to forgive is that it was not "plan B" or an after thought on His part. His forgiveness towards us was not a response to mankind's failure to obey Him. This choice was well thought out and made even before any of creation occurred. Just think about it. Before God even began to speak the created order into existence, He considered man from His character of love and chose to forgive! Listen to what the scripture says about this. In Revelation 13: 8b it says, "… the Lamb (Jesus) slain from the foundation of the world." The preposition "from" can be interpreted as "before." Paul clearly demonstrates this choice of forgiveness by stating in Ephesians 1: 4a, "Just as He chose us in Him before the foundation of the world…" Yes, thanks be to God, He chose to forgive us! When it comes to forgiving one another, there must be an act of our will to choose to forgive. This is just like God in Christ chose to forgive us.

Jesus not only chose to forgive us, He also suffered to forgive us! As the writer of Hebrews is discussing how to continue on in our faith in chapter 12, he mentions something of Christ's suffering in verse 2 that secured our forgiveness. " Looking unto Jesus, the author and finisher of our faith, who for the joy that was set before Him endured the cross, despising the shame, and has sat down at the right hand of the throne of God." In the book of Isaiah, chapter 53, we find a dramatic presentation of the suffering of Jesus Christ for the sins of all the world. The sin problem of the human race required a sacrifice beyond what any man who will ever live, besides Christ could provide. Jesus is the perfect Lamb of God who takes away the sin of the world. And the only way sin could be removed was through the shedding of His blood and the giving of His life. Hebrews 9:22 indicates, " And without shedding of blood, there is no remission," or another word for "remission" is forgiveness. This great sacrifice of suffering is an example again of how God in Christ forgave.

Suffering is not easy. There is pain involved. It is uncomfortable, but often times forgiveness requires a measure of suffering. Remember that forgiveness is not associated with satisfaction but with a sense of release. This may result in some satisfaction or peace but not necessarily. Releasing someone from your bitter judgment can be quite painful and difficult. I have witnessed numerous individuals go through considerable suffering in reaching this point. But we cannot allow pain to keep us from truly expressing love towards someone. Loving one another means to forgive them and as I stated earlier, forgiving one another is the main ingredient of what it means to love others.

Years ago, I sustained an injury to my left knee that required about 20 stitches. An infection set in the wound days later that continued to grow. The tenderness and pain when I would touch it was horrible, but I learned to live with it the best I could. The wound healed but the infection remained. As long as I didn't touch it, bang it, or think too much about it, I was fine. The time came to remove the stitches and when the doctor saw the knee he just shook his head. He said, "I'm going to have to cut your knee open to get the infection out." My response was, "Over my dead body!" Just to touch it hurt, to think about cutting it open was too much to consider. To leave it alone would eventually create a serious condition that could require the removal of the leg or even loss of my own life. Compared to that, cutting the wound open again even though it would be quite painful was a better alternative. So I gave my consent to perform the procedure. Yes you're right, it hurt and yes, I cried like a baby! But I still have my life and leg today!

Forgiving one another will at times be painful. Getting revenge appeals to our fleshly nature and seems like it would be more satisfying, but loving one another like Jesus wants us to demands forgiveness. In the long run, we all know it is the best choice even though suffering is involved.

The third feature of this description of forgiveness is that He continues to forgive. In a purely theological sense, on the cross all of our sins were forgiven. This includes the sins of the world. As we find ourselves in Christ, we are able to appropriate that forgiveness. The appropriation of this forgiveness is found in the present when we take responsibility for our actions and trusting in the finished work of Jesus on the cross, we ask for and choose to receive forgiveness from Him. The continual activity on the part of God in Christ is simply releasing forgiveness into our lives when we ask. This free provision of forgiveness is totally based on the complete and finished work of Christ on the cross. The Apostle John says it best in his first epistle:

"This is the message which we have heard from Him and declare to you, that God is light and in Him is no darkness at all. If we say that we have fellowship with Him, and walk in darkness, we lie and do not practice the truth. But if we walk in the light as He is in the light, we have fellowship with one another, and the blood of Jesus Christ His Son cleanses us from all sin. If we say that we have no sin, we deceive ourselves, and the truth is not in us. If we confess our sins, He is faithful and just to forgive us our sins and to cleanse us from all unrighteousness. If we say that we have not sinned, we make Him a liar, and His word is not in us. My little children, these things I write to you, so that you may not sin. And if anyone sins, we have an Advocate with the Father, Jesus Christ the righteous. And He Himself is the propitiation for our sins, and not for ours only but also for the whole world" (1John 1:5-2:2).

John is clearly describing the continual work of God in forgiving us! Because of the sacrifice already made, forgiveness is available for everyone and not just at certain times. It is available 24/7 as long as we have breath in our bodies!

The application of this description is quite clear. Forgiveness is not something we should be holding out on one another. There are no certain conditions or particular rituals one needs to go through in order to "merit" our forgiveness of them. God commands us to be a forgiving people and this "forgiving" verb is in the present tense, indicating the habitual, continual nature of the action. This is not to be occasional or whenever it feels "right" to forgive. Forgiveness is to be a continual action on our part, just like God in Christ has forgiven us.

So, there we have it. God chose to forgive us, suffered to forgive us and continues to forgive us. The insights from these concepts provide an accurate picture of what God is expecting of us. As we consider this description of what forgiveness looks like, may God give us the grace to begin living it out!

The Action of Forgiveness Demonstrated

Now, we come to the part where the "rubber hits the road." It's one thing to define and describe forgiveness; it's another to demonstrate it! Of course, without the demonstration realized, all you have is theory and fancy words and concepts. Forgiving one another is not just a belief held by Christians, it is the main ingredient of loving others! It is to be interwoven throughout the relationships we have with one another. The intent of this action in Christian relationships is a regularly occurring experience. Our previous discussion defined and described forgiveness, so we know what it is. The question before us now is, "How do we show it or demonstrate it?"

There are two particular passages in the Gospel of Matthew that answer this question. Both of these passages are Jesus' specific teachings about how to walk in a forgiving way towards others. One is Matthew 5: 23-24:

"Therefore if you bring your gift to the altar, and there remember that your brother has something against you, leave your gift there before the altar, and go your way. First be reconciled to your brother, and then come and offer your gift."

The other passage is Matthew 18:15-17:

"Moreover if your brother sins against you, go and tell him his fault between you and him alone. If he hears you, you have gained your brother. But if he will not hear, take with you one or two more, that by the mouth of two or three witnesses every word may be established. And if he refuses to hear them, tell it to the church. But if he refuses even to hear the church, let him be to you like a heathen and a tax collector."

I must say that in the 30 plus years that I've been in the ministry, I have witnessed every perversion of these scriptures imaginable. Often, only parts of these verses are used in order to justify the sinful and evil actions of individuals seeking to direct, instruct, correct, or simply to control others. I have personally experienced seeing church leaders literally twisting these verses around in order to give credence to their prideful and jealous hearts in order to destroy other Christians and leaders in their church. The wounding of so many Christians from misapplication or just plain ignorance of these passages has emptied many church pews! What is so sad is that if we only understood what forgiveness is about and how to actually live forgiving one another, the opposite response would happen, churches would be overflowing with people because they would be loved! Well then, let's carefully glean from these passages of scripture how to demonstrate forgiveness!

It is interesting to note first that Jesus directs for action to take place on our parts regardless of who did what. Whether we offended someone or were offended by someone, no matter what the case, we are commanded by our Lord to move into action. And this action called for is the same whether we are offended or the one who offended another. There are three actions important enough to discuss here.

The first action is actually implied based on the entire concept of forgiveness as I explained earlier. This action is to forgive first! No matter what our feelings or thoughts may be about the matter, we need to forgive one another in our hearts before any other action takes place. If we don't release someone from our bitter judgment from the beginning within our heart, then we will go with the wrong attitude. We may be only secretly desiring our "pound of flesh." We may only be trying to justify, minimize, or rationalize ourselves in the matter. There could possibly be an attitude of condemnation toward a person or just bad thoughts and feelings that won't go away no matter how much they say or agree with us. As we are able to forgive in our hearts first, we can go with the right attitude seeking the best possible solution for the difficulty. Even if the solution is not the most beneficial to "me." Forgiving first means you go with no hidden motives or agendas. Your one desire is to restore the relationship in love in the safest environment you can provide for this experience to take place, if at all possible.

THE FORGOTTEN COMMANDMENT

I know of one pastor who was accused by several individuals who had actually collaborated together before making the accusations. The accusations were quite minor but because of the number of individuals involved, it appeared to be a bigger problem. The entire situation was based on offenses in the work place that were never properly expressed or attempts made to deal with. The offenses in the accuser's hearts turned to bitterness and hatred and then were expressed to the dismay of many. Unfortunately, the leadership around the pastor had their own unexpressed and unresolved negative issues. These "leaders" were inexperienced and ill trained individuals that horribly mishandled the situation. When these folks got together, it was like gasoline and fire that resulted in many wounded believers. The desire on the part of the accusers was to extract their "pound of flesh" (which is never fully gained) and to demoralize and demonize the pastor in the community. If only they would have forgiven first, possibly a great revival might have occurred in that small community. We must learn to forgive first!

The second action is directly indicated from the scripture passages. It is to take the initiative and go! Again, whether you offended another or are the offended party, you are to take the first step and go to the other person. Too often I see individuals going through life overlooking offenses they inflicted on others thinking they have good reasons for their actions. There is no sense of responsibility experienced on their part to seek to correct the situation. They feel justified or have rationalized their position. To consider going to the person they offended and resolving the issue according to this teaching about forgiveness and placing a loving relationship with that person as the higher priority, isn't given a second thought. I believe they think, "What's important is my position and the matter of me being right! If anyone is going to take the first step it needs to be the person who is in the "wrong" and by the way, they need to crawl when they come." At this point, I believe they need to go back to the chapter on kindness and spend time digesting that material again.

On the other hand, I see individuals carrying around deep offenses in their hearts, some for years. They seem convinced that the person who offended them needs to take action first and come asking for forgiveness. Unless this occurs, the offense remains in the heart and unfortunately, the hurt transforms into bitterness, resentment, and hatred. Jesus clearly explains in these scriptures that you demonstrate forgiveness, no matter what, take the first step of action and go. I know, I know, this is not easy, but this is God's love in action through us!

In both passages, Jesus says to "go." This Greek word for go is quite interesting to examine. For one thing, it is not the usual word for coming and going. This particular word Jesus uses carries the meaning of going with a purpose in mind. The indication here is that you don't just go to go and see what might happen, but you go with a committed and clear purpose to accomplish a goal. That goal is reconciliation back to the best loving relationship possible. It is understandable that everything may not be like it used to be, but the attempt and goal is to make the best possible relationship occur. The important matter here is not proving who is the most right or wrong or how much you can make the other person crawl and make you feel superior, it is about restoring a loving relationship again. Oh! If we could only get this in our thick heads!

Another interesting feature about this word "go" is that it is in the present tense. As previously explained, the present tense in the Greek indicates the continual action of the word. We are to go and keep on going. In other words, a serious attempt is to occur. This is not just to be a one-time experience and if it's not successful then "let's deal harshly or kick this person out of the church!" Tender loving care should be expressed along with patient long suffering. Remember the goal in going, to bring about a loving relationship, not proving right and wrongness or extracting the confession of sin. This only breeds contempt and releases a spirit of accusation and condemnation resulting in relational disaster among many.

The third action is blended into the first two and is clearly delineated by Jesus. When we go, we are to go privately. This action is about meeting privately for the purpose of reconciliation. I hear so often, "I can't go by myself. It won't do any good," or "I'm afraid to do this alone, I need others to give me support in order to work through this." The scripture is clear that if you try numerous times on your own and reconciliation is not accomplished, then you can involve one or two other people at the most to assist. Usually there are dozens of people who know and are emotionally involved before anything is attempted. Now the spirit of accusation and condemnation is rampant and the entire situation is a mess. Very seldom in 30 years of ministry have I ever seen a situation be resolved with reconciliation and loving relationships resulting when others are involved too soon. Jesus provides a distinctive plan to follow and there are no alternatives. We either follow His specific plan or we will produce a relational crisis or disaster!

The involvement of other people before the appropriate time is a direct indication that reconciliation and restoring a loving relationship is not the goal in sight. The goal manifested in this is justification of one party and condemnation of the other. This is the "I'm right and you're wrong" mindset.

The goal of forgiveness and restoring a loving relationship can best be facilitated through private meetings. As long as the situation involves only two people there is less chance of further misunderstandings, half-truths being perpetuated, and justification/condemnation issues becoming the focus of thought and attention. I believe in all of my research and experiences with people that nearly 80% of the offenses and difficulties between people are simply the result of misunderstanding or unmet expectations. For the most part, people are not intentionally setting out to harm and wound others.

Misjudging the motives of others is a common experience. Often given the time alone discussing the matter in a spirit of forgiveness and love, the majority of offenses are cleared up and positive reconciliation occurs. But I must emphasize that we need to follow Jesus' command to go privately before involving others.

I believe it's worth the time to quickly review. The pattern laid out by Jesus is three-fold. First, forgive in your heart releasing the person from your bitter judgment before going. Second, go with a committed purpose to reconcile with the person even if it takes numerous attempts. Third, as you do go, do it privately, keeping the whole matter confidential between the person and yourself. This plan is the only way offenses can be resolved and relationships can be restored to God's standard.

The question arises in my mind, "What if after forgiveness is properly given, the person offends, again even repeatedly?" What are we to do? Consideration of the demonstration of forgiveness requires us to examine one other point of action to answer this question. There is another teaching of Jesus we must examine to direct our thoughts. This teaching is found in Matthew 18:21-35.

"Then Peter came to Him and said, 'Lord, how often shall my brother sin against me, and I forgive him? Up to seven times?' Jesus said to him, 'I do not say to you, up to seven times, but up to seventy times seven. Therefore the kingdom of heaven is like a certain king who wanted to settle accounts with his servants. And when he had begun to settle accounts, one was brought to him who owed him ten thousand talents. But as he was not able to pay, his master commanded that he be sold, with his wife and children and all that he had, and that payment be made. The servant therefore fell down before him, saying, "Master, have patience with me, and I will pay you all." Then the master of that servant was moved with compassion, released him, and forgave him the debt.

But that servant went out and found one of his fellow servants who owed him a hundred denarii; and he laid hands on him and took him by the throat, saying, "Pay me what you owe." So his fellow servant fell down at his feet and begged him, saying, "Have patience with me, and I will pay you all." And he would not, but went and threw him into prison til he should pay the debt. So when his fellow servants saw what had been done, they were very grieved, and came and told their master all that had been done. Then his master, after he had called him, said to him, "You wicked servant! I forgave you all that debt because you begged me, Should you have not also had compassion on your fellow servant, just as I had pity on you?" And his master was angry, and delivered him to the torturers until he should pay all that was due to him.

So My heavenly Father also will do to you if each of you, from his heart, does not forgive his brother his trespasses.

Wow! This is another powerful teaching from Jesus. The Lord is providing for us out of this passage what might be thought of as an ongoing attitude about this whole matter of forgiveness. Rather than dealing with offense as it happens, Jesus is telling us to have this attitude as we go through life. This attitude embraces forgiveness as unconditional, unlimited, and as possessing quality.

The question the disciples ask Jesus is quite interesting to look at. Historians tell us that the going rate of the Rabbis regarding forgiveness was that if you forgave three times than you were exhibiting great godliness. When Peter speaks to Jesus, it appears as if he doubles the rate and adds one more for good measure, thinking he might impress Jesus. Actually, according to the current standards of the time, his question does sound quite generous. But Jesus' response is astonishing! Seven times seventy is light-years beyond what anyone would have guessed. It would be foolish to think Jesus was indicating that the actual number of 490 was now the godly number of how many times in a day one should forgive.

Seven in the Jewish understanding represented fullness or completion. Seventy represents completion to eternity. So Jesus was directly revealing that forgiveness needed to be an attitude we carried around in our hearts that would include the characteristics of serious quality, an unlimited number, and a sense of being unconditional. In other words, there is no limitation or variable that would determine when we are no longer to forgive. Forgiveness is like a river that continually flows in our hearts towards one another. The basis for this is found in the story Jesus tells in the passage.

Putting the amounts found in the scripture into modern-day vernacular helps in the understanding. The master in the story actually releases the servant of about $10,000,000. That's right, ten million dollars! How this man got into such debt we are not told. We only know he was so deeply in debt that he would never be able to pay it back. The master forgives him of that which he could never repay, absolutely amazing! But even more amazing is that this servant walks away from this experience and comes across a man who owes him $20. The servant wants his money and refuses to forgive the debt for any reason. No matter what the man says, it's not good enough. The ending result is that the servant is brought back to the master who cannot fathom why he would not forgive the debt of the other man so the servant is severely punished.

This passage does remind us of the importance of forgiving (releasing someone from our bitter judgment). If there is a grudge in our hearts, then when a person sins again, it only adds to the unforgiveness dwelling deep inside and so we experience heightened negative feelings towards the person. We might even think or say, "I forgave once or twice, but this is it! I'm not forgiving again!"

It is a difficult fact to face but the above scenario indicates not only a lack of genuine forgiveness to begin with but even more serious is that this indicates an attitude of what I call an "all about me" mindset. The thing that is really most important is what happens to "me" and how something affects "me." Once true forgiveness as already described is expressed, then future sins of the same nature are dealt with as individual sins and not a compilation of continuing occurrences. In other words, you're not keeping score and holding secret grudges.

Understand this is not to be an excuse for someone's sinful behavior either. A continual sin problem is evidence of deeper needs that should be addressed through the proper channels and with the involvement of professionals who can provide help. Unfortunately, experience has demonstrated reactions by Christians and churches that are not constructive and usually result in wounded people on both sides of the fence. Following Christ's admonitions and the understanding from this teaching will give positive direction and a higher potential for better outcomes.

The illustration given by the Lord here demonstrates that those (who include everyone of us) who receive His forgiveness should be willing to forgive anyone else no matter what the particulars are. Because we receive maximum mercy from the Lord, we should in turn show mercy to others. What others do to us is only a small fraction in comparison to what each of us has done to Jesus! We are the benefactors of such great mercy, who are we to demand justice in another? Who do we think we are to demand accounts due? We are to do the same as God has done to us. Anything else would demonstrate pure hypocrisy on our parts! This sure does make the picture look different than when we first began. Taking seriously this matter of loving one another means we must have as the main ingredient of our love, forgiving one another just like Christ has forgiven us! This is what we are called to do. This is what God expects from every Christian. Let's commit ourselves to begin living this feature of love immediately!

The Action of Forgiveness for Difficult Situations

The elderly pastor was searching his closet for his collar before church one Sunday morning. In the back of the closet, he found a small box containing three eggs and 100 one-dollar bills. He called his wife into the closet to ask her about the box and it's contents. Embarrassed, she admitted having hidden the box there for the entire 25 years of marriage. Disappointed and hurt, the pastor asked her, "Why?" The wife replied, " I didn't want to hurt your feelings." He asked her how the box might hurt his feelings. She said that every time during their marriage that he had delivered a poor sermon, she had placed an egg in the box.

The pastor felt that three poor sermons in 25 years was certainly nothing to feel bad about, so he asked her what the 100 one dollar bills were for. She replied, "Each time I got a dozen eggs, I sold them to the neighbors for $1."

Ouch! As Jesus told us, offenses will come. They often come from those closest to us. The hard truth is that in real life, situations can occur that may make this whole process appear quite complicated.

It is natural for various questions to arise in your mind at this point regarding some very difficult situations you may personally be facing or can think of. Some say to me, "Yes, I believe what you're teaching is the truth and should be followed, but you just don't understand my particular situation. You're talking about what can occur in an ideal world only!" It is true that forgiving one another like God forgives us is not an easy thing to do. If it were, there would not be the need for this teaching or for the power of the Holy Spirit working in our lives. Everyone would just be doing it with no problem. But the truth of the matter is that forgiveness is a real problem in the church and millions of Christians are spiritually crippled and paralyzed because of it. For too long the Christian world has ignored and pretended to love one another without forgiveness as described in this teaching being a part of their "love." The result is an impotent church and a world in darkness crying out for a real expression of God to see!

Well then, let's spend a little time addressing some of the difficult situations and provide strategies to successfully navigate through them. The first difficulty that comes to my mind is what about when someone else doesn't see the offense like you do. Although you have gone over and over in your mind all of the events and it seems so clear to you, when you present it, the other person has a totally different version. This is what we can identify as a perception problem.

In considering this, we must understand that things are not always like you or the other person perceives them. We all have our own filters in our minds that events process through. Often these processes are complicated and past experiences and environmental factors can cause us to perceive situations in ways that may not be necessarily correct with all the facts. Evidence of this struggle is witnessed everyday when many people may see a crime committed and when the police examines each witness, several versions of the events emerge. They all saw the same thing but they all experience it individually. This results in the multiple stories supplied. No one is deliberately lying, they all feel their version is completely accurate. It is the processing of our brains through these "filters" mentioned that create the different versions. So, it is very possible that our version of what occurred in the offense may be inaccurate and possibly totally off base.

This of course will be hard to reconcile if either of you are absolutely convinced your version is the only one correct. Working through this difficulty requires an open mind and a willingness to reconcile as most important. Remember, you're not supposed to be out for a "pound of flesh," you're interested in forgiveness to take place. If you have forgiven first to begin with, that will lessen the potential problems that can arise from this difficulty. This is really a part of the strategy here in that you are most interested in restoring the relationship. You should let them know you felt hurt regardless of the situation (your perception of the events resulted in your hurt feelings) and then let them know you have forgiven them no matter what they might say and you want to accept them in restoring the relationship. For the most part, this will solve the majority of situations. If this doesn't work, the next part of the strategy is simply to leave it all with the Lord! You are responsible for you and your actions only. How someone else reacts or responds is their business before the Lord. I think of the scripture in Proverbs chapter three where we are told, " Trust in the Lord with all of your heart and lean not unto your own understanding. In all of your ways acknowledge Him and He will direct your paths." Leaving something with the Lord means to leave it with the Lord, period!

There is a second difficult situation worth mentioning. This is when you make attempts to deal with the offense and the situation gets worse! It might just remain the same regardless of what you say or do. Either they refuse to forgive you or take any responsibility for the offense involved. As with the first difficult situation, there are three parts of the strategy to incorporate. To begin with, carefully check your own attitude and the spirit you have been going and discussing the matter with the other person. Without forgiving first as previously discussed, you might be going with a sense of judgment wanting that "pound of flesh." No matter how strong or spiritually mature you may think you are, if you haven't forgiven first, negative attitudes will creep into your relating with another. The case may even require you receive some professional help in forgiving first before you can actually attempt reconciliation.

I have seen so many times Christians make terrible mistakes at this point. Instead of dealing with their own wounds and receiving inner healing and other forms of professional help, they engage the "help" of the wrong people. Often, going to your pastor is not the answer because so many pastors are untrained and ill equipped to handle these problems. Just because they can preach a good sermon doesn't mean they are capable of helping in this difficulty. I personally witnessed a pastor of a rather large congregation horribly injure untold individuals and families because he thought he possessed the skills necessary for dealing with offenses between people. Memories still linger in my mind of how unprofessional and incapable he was as he deeply hurt multitudes. The point here is not to just assume your pastor or your "best friend" has the capacity for helping you through this process. Take the time to find the right person if you cannot forgive first.

Now, after you have gone many times to seek reconciliation and nothing positive is resulting, then follow the scripture admonition to take an elder or two with you to help. Be sure you understand this involvement of elders is only if all parties involved are in the same church. If there are individuals outside the life of the church you might have to skip this step all together or involve an individual or two in leadership capacity over the other person in the world they are operating in. You see, this whole matter of reconciliation has to do with the life and welfare of the church. It's more about the fellowship within the body of Christ than about you and your feelings and satisfaction of justice. This is a very important point we must never lose sight of.

The last part of this strategy is the same as with the first one. Leave it with the Lord. When we feel unsuccessful in our attempts, we may not fully understand what the Lord is up to in all of this. It might be the best thing to just leave it in the Lord's hands and allow Him to deal with it in His time and purpose. If we have truly forgiven first, this will not be a hard thing to do. We never know what God is up to. Our many efforts may actually frustrate the will of God in some situations. Again, leave it to the Lord, He is fully capable of handling every situation!

The third difficult situation has to do if the other person involved in the offense is deceased. For some believers, by the time they are ready to deal with offenses, the person who offended them is gone, passed away. I find this scenario with individuals who seek counseling and uncover negative incidents from their past. What do you do when you can no longer confront or talk with another because they are deceased? Again the strategy is three-fold.

Remember the idea of forgiving first. This is the thread interwoven throughout all matters of forgiveness. This will provide many solutions to what may seem insurmountable odds. Keep this foremost in your thinking and actions.

The three-fold strategy begins with talking with someone you trust. Although you cannot speak to the deceased person, you can discuss the whole matter with another trustworthy individual. This may begin the healing process.

Next, you need to settle the matter in your heart. This might include some ritual or activity on your part like writing a letter, going to a grave site, or something else to help you in producing closure regarding the offense. Whatever you choose to do, the important matter is to settle it in your heart.

The final piece of the strategy is to leave it with the Lord. As with the other difficult situations, sometimes the last point of peace will come when we leave it in God's hands. After all, He is big enough to take care of all matters sufficiently. We need to believe this. In other words, our concept of who God is and what He is up to in our lives and the universe needs to include His capacity for knowing what is best for every situation. In this we must trust and leave all offenses in His hands. I am reminded of the precious song, "He's got the whole world in His hands." He does and we must learn to trust Him!

I am sure there will be other difficult situations not addressed here in this work. But the principles found here can easily be translated for just about every situation you may find yourself in. The two principles most important to apply are forgiving first and leaving it with the Lord. I'm sure you could have guessed those with no problem. I hope you are able to see the enormous value contained in this section of material and will seek to devote yourself to living this matter of forgiveness "out loud" in your Christian life!

The Action of Forgiveness Discarded

The final point to discuss on this entire section on forgiveness has to do with the potential option we all have about choosing **not to forgive**. Although you might think this is not an option after all we have discussed, the truth of the matter is many do choose not to forgive. For whatever reasons, and people have many, the choice not to forgive is many more times chosen than to walk through the processes described in this book. Maybe it seems too painful or for another purpose, but some choose to discard the action of forgiveness.

What we need to do is to consider what the consequences are for discarding the act to love and forgive because they are grave! There are two specific teachings of Jesus addressing these consequences that must be known. The consequences themselves might even provide the motivation to reconsider the choice to forgive. Let's carefully examine each one.

The first one is found in Matthew 6: 14-15. Read the scripture first:

"For if you forgive men their trespasses, your heavenly Father will also forgive you. But if you do not forgive men their trespasses, neither will your Father forgive your trespasses."

This is a familiar passage to many. It is included in what often is called the Lord's Prayer, but actually it is Jesus' teaching to His disciples about how believers should pray. It could be more accurately called the disciple's prayer. Jesus covers a number of very important topics to give attention to in praying. It is significant that after Jesus gives the prayer, He regresses for a moment in order to focus again on one of the topics, forgiveness. What Jesus states here is quite astonishing and dramatically illustrates the consequences of refusing to forgive. Discarding the commandment to forgive will result in the inability to obtain forgiveness for yourself. This is really quite devastating for several reasons.

Knowing you are forgiven is paramount in the Christian's life. To consider the potential of living without God's forgiveness is scary! The alternative is to live in sin. Living in sin opens the spiritual door for darkness to enter and influence your life. In addition, you can be affected psychologically. Your thoughts and feelings are intricately connected to your spiritual condition and unforgiveness often breeds negativity within them. Unforgiveness easily turns into bitterness that is compared to cancer in the emotional being. It can slowly deteriorate and destroy your

THE FORGOTTEN COMMANDMENT

sense of well-being. The foundation to peace and joy in the Christian's life flows out of the knowledge and experience of forgiveness.

But you may object, "Now wait a minute! Are you saying God won't forgive any of my sins if I choose not to forgive just one thing another has done to me?" Yes I am! But realize Jesus said it first! This is why this matter of forgiving one another is so vital.

Consider with me for a moment the dynamics of unforgiveness. Choosing not to forgive is actually an expression of pride where you take God's place in a given situation and this is sin in itself. God has chosen to forgive everyone in Christ. The sacrifice of Jesus Christ on the cross is adequate to cover the sins of the entire world. He has taken the place of everyone. He has suffered the punishment and penalty for every person so that forgiveness can be given freely. This forgiveness is not only what God can give to us but also what we can give to others.

When we come to Christ, we are to give up our personal rights and place our lives under the Lordship of Christ. Refusing to forgive another is basically an unwillingness to give up our rights. We are essentially declaring that Christ's death was not sufficient to cover this offense and more "blood" must be shed (this pound of flesh idea again), usually on the part of the offender. This whole direction of thought reveals the sheer ungodliness and evil trail a person is traveling. As long as you're on this trail, you are outside the fellowship and blessing of God in Christ. So, you are living in rebellion to God's command to love and forgive and so you can never know you're forgiven, you are in sin! Shocking! Most of us never consider this.

I am reminded of a story about a retired marine drill sergeant and his three sons. The sons were 14, 11, and 9 years old. The old sergeant had a whistle he carried around his neck and would blow when he wanted his boys to appear on the scene. They would come running and all stand at attention waiting for their father's orders.

One day the boys were playing ball out in the yard and accidentally, the ball came crashing in through the living room window. Extremely disturbed, the father blew the whistle several times. Immediately the boys ran into the house and all stood at attention before their father as he one-eyed each one of them. Finally with the ball in his hand, he stepped up right in the face of the oldest son and whipped, "Son, do you know anything about this ball that come through that window and busted that window Boy?" Not missing a beat the eldest son quickly responded, "No sir! I don't know anything about that ball come through that window and busted that window sir!" The father stepped directly down the line to the second son and stated the same question holding the ball in his hand. The second boy quickly responded in the same manner as the first boy. The father then moved in front of the youngest boy getting nose-to-nose and yelling the same question. By this time, the youngest son was trembling as he attempted to answer his father. He said, "Yes sir! I know something about that ball that come through the window and busted that window sir! And I want a transfer out of this chicken outfit!"

When you're in the Lord's army, there's no transferring out! It is not optional to follow His commandments. We don't get to choose which ones we will obey and the ones we won't. Being a Christian means we are to love one another and the main ingredient of loving one another is forgiving one another like God forgives us. Not to do this is to place ourselves in a place where we can never know forgiveness!

The second teaching of Jesus is found in Matthew 18:21-35. Take a look at this scripture again.

"Then Peter came to Him and said, 'Lord, how often shall my brother sin against me, and I forgive him? Up to seven times?' Jesus said to him, 'I do not say to you, up to seven times, but up to seventy times seven. Therefore the kingdom of heaven is like a certain king who wanted to settle accounts with his servants. And when he had begun to settle accounts, one was brought to him who owed him ten thousand talents. But as he was not able to pay, his master commanded that he be sold, with his wife and children and all that he had, and that payment be made. The servant therefore fell down before him, saying, "Master, have patience with me, and I will pay you all." Then the master of that servant was moved with compassion, released him, and forgave him the debt.

But that servant went out and found one of his fellow servants who owed him a hundred denarii; and he laid hands on him and took him by the throat, saying, "Pay me what you owe." So his fellow servant fell down at his feet and begged him, saying, "Have patience with me, and I will pay you all." And he would not, but went and threw him into prison til he should pay the debt. So when his fellow servants saw what had been done, they were very grieved, and came and told their master all that had been done. Then his master, after he had called him, said to him, "You wicked servant! I forgave you all that debt because you begged me, Should you have not also had compassion on your fellow servant, just as I had pity on you?" And his master was angry, and delivered him to the torturers until he should pay all that was due to him.

So My heavenly Father also will do to you if each of you, from his heart, does not forgive his brother his trespasses.

I believe that verse 35 in this text is the most shocking verse in the entire New Testament! With tremendous clarity, Jesus is declaring that when you choose not to forgive then our heavenly Father will turn us over to the "torturers." The "torturers" in this passage speak of those who are experts in the use of the rack, a horrible form of torture. The correlation to our situations would be that we would be turned over to demons to be tormented. In other words, when we choose not to forgive, we will experience inner torment! The demonic spirits of anger, resentment, hatred, bitterness, revenge, just to name a few, will have free course in our lives to wreak havoc with our emotions and thinking processes. It is no wonder how some individuals suffering from chronic mental illnesses have deep roots of unforgiveness within them.

This is an area of serious consideration. I have seen more Christians than I want to be shipwrecked in their walk with the Lord because of bitterness and unforgiveness. Once there were signs of spiritual life like joy, peace, love, and spiritual direction in their lives, but now they seem like an empty shell. They may still go through the motions of Christian life, but there is no longer the life that once characterized them. Usually they only have words of blame and shame towards those they refuse to forgive, all the time in inner torment. Some have even developed an entire thought process of justification as to the way they think, feel, and live, almost enjoying a sense of the darkness and bitterness they exist in. It is a shame and a disgrace to the Lord.

You might say at this point," Is this supported by other teachings in the New Testament?" Yes it is. The Apostle Paul clearly warns us to be careful not to provide an opportunity or a place for demons to gain a foothold into our life. In 2 Corinthians 2: 10-11, Paul tells us if we give them a place, they will take it and use it as an advantage over our lives. This opportunity or place we can give a demon is unforgiveness.

We never solve any relational problem by refusing to forgive. In this scenario, all experience hurt and pain. This hinders even the kingdom itself. It's time to examine our hearts and make sure that there is no unforgiveness lingering around in us!

There were two old-time comedians that demonstrated this concept in one of their routines. The "dumb-one" of the two shows up one day with a stick of dynamite strapped to his chest. The other one says, "Hey, what are you doing with that dynamite strapped to your chest?" The "dumb-one" responded, "You know old Joe? Every time he comes around, he walks up to me and slaps me on my chest. It really hurts me and I'm tired of him doing that. The next time he slaps me on the chest, I'm gonna blow his hand off!"

When we choose not to forgive one another we might "blow their hand off" but we end up blowing our heart out! We are the ones who will suffer the most. We are the ones who have to face the consequences of our Heavenly Father turning us over for inner torment. Let's choose right now to forgive, forgive, and forgive. Let it be the main ingredient in our love for others!

Well, that about wraps it up! Forgiveness is a serious matter to God and He desires for us to make it just as serious in our lifestyle. In learning what it really means to love one another, we must clearly understand that forgiving is the main ingredient in this love. Thank God, He demonstrated His love toward us in this way and we should follow suit! One of the greatest decisions you can make for your own welfare is to live out this kind of love, both towards yourself and others. When we forgive like God in Christ forgives us, then the love of God truly is alive in us!

It would be worthwhile to set this book aside right now and search our hearts to see if there is any unforgiveness abiding in us. Let's choose to forgive, forgive, and keep on forgiving!

Chapter Outline for Preaching or Teaching
(2 Messages)

FORGIVING ONE ANOTHER (Col. 3:13 Eph. 4:32)

Introduction: Forgiving one another is the main ingredient in the whole matter of loving one another. As we begin to draw closer together as a church family, we will need to understand what forgiving one another is really all about!

I. **The Action of Forgiveness Defined and Described**
1. Forgiveness defined
    (1) The Greek word "chridzomai" means "giving grace."
    (2) What forgiveness is **not**.
    (3) This verb is in the present tense.
    (4) This verb is in the imperative mode.
    (5) This verb is in the middle voice.

2. Forgiveness Described
    (1) Jesus choose to do it!
    (2) *Jesus suffered to do it!*
    (3) Jesus continues to do it!

II. **The Action of Forgiveness Demonstrated**
1. What Jesus teaches us about forgiveness in the Gospel of Matthew

    (1) Forgive first.
    (2) Take the initiative and go.
    (3) Deal with others privately for the purpose of reconciliation.

2. Ongoing attitude of forgiveness.

Conclusion: We are the recipients of maximum mercy and grace who are we to give others anything less?

FORGIVING ONE ANOTHER (Part 2)

Introduction: Forgiving one another is at the very heart of what it means to love one another. When we consider the meaning of the Greek word for forgiveness, it leaves us with a focus on our own lives in the way we choose to deal with ourselves long before we begin to focus on others. But there are some difficult questions and situations that arise....

I. THE ACTION OF FORGIVENESS FOR DIFFICULT SITUATIONS

1. What if they do not see it like you do?

    (1) Things are not always like you perceive them.
    (2) Let them know you felt hurt and forgive them in restoring the relationship.
    (3) Leave it to the Lord.

2. What if the situation gets worse or remains the same?

    (1) Carefully check your own attitude and the spirit you are going with.
    (2) Take an elder with you, if they're in your church.
    (3) Leave it to the Lord.

3. What if the person is deceased?

    (1) Talk with someone you trust.
    (2) Settle the matter in your heart.
    (3) Leave it to the Lord.

II. THE ACTION OF FORGIVENESS DISCARDED

1. You can never know forgiveness. Matt. 6:14-15

2. You will experience inner torment. Matt. 18:35

Conclusion: Forgiveness is of great importance with God. What are you going to do????

Group Study Questions

1. Share a meaningful experience in forgiving someone. Also share one about being forgiven.

2. How do you understand forgiveness as the main ingredient of love?

3. How does the chapter define what forgiveness means?

4. Why do you think some people have a hard time forgiving? How can you help them?

5. Why do you think some people have such a hard time forgiving themselves?

6. What is the goal of forgiveness and how does it fit into God's plan for believers?

7. What is the most important thing you learned from the chapter?

CHAPTER SIX

Rejoicing and Weeping With One Another
(Romans 12:15)

The Fourth of July weekend was approaching and the preschool teacher took the opportunity to discuss patriotism with her class. "We live in a great country," she said. "One of the things we should be happy is that in this country, we are all free." One little boy came walking up to her from the back of the room. He stood with his hands on his hips and said, "I'm not free, I'm four!"

It seems to me that after 30 plus years of being a Christian and teaching these truths for a long time, I would have got it together by now but I'm still just scratching the surface. Oh, the depths of the riches of knowing Christ and allowing Him to live His life through me! It makes the Christian life the most exciting way to live on the earth. You never get bored or finish the course. We are all on a journey that is continuous and full of wonderful treasures to discover and experience! Learning to love one another is the most important element in following Christ and opens up the riches and the power of God in us. When I think about rejoicing and weeping with one another, I believe these are the activities of love.

Love is a verb. It is full of action. The other aspects of loving one another already considered do imply action of some kind, but rejoicing and weeping are specific actions that lead our relationships with others to the deepest level imaginable. These two elements in action between believers truly enhance and liberate relationships to their deepest and greatest potential. Learning to rejoice and weep with one another sets in motion the dynamics for this growth in love to occur!

Rejoicing With One Another

Let's first turn our attention to this matter of rejoicing with one another. The Apostle Paul simply but profoundly states, "Rejoice with those who rejoice." It is so brief a statement that we might easily pass right by not noticing the importance of the verse. But as we have seen in other verses related to loving one another, these small portions of scripture contain tremendously pregnant truth! Our strategy here is to examine the definition, description, and the difficulties of rejoicing with one another, so let's begin!

The Definition of Rejoicing With One Another

The Greek word for rejoice is "chairo." This word indicates a matter of being exceedingly glad, full of cheer, and to be delighted openly and expressively. You might even say this word expresses real happiness (something everyone in the world is looking for). When you consider this from that angle, we should figure out a way to package this and sell it. We'd make a fortune! It is so interesting to me that one of the things most desired by all of mankind (to be happy) is wrapped up in such a neat little package.

Do you realize that the shortest verse in the entire Bible communicates this very same message? You ask, where is it?" The shortest verse in the entire Bible is found in 1 Thessalonians 5:16. It says, "Rejoice always." In the Greek, this verse is only one word! This is the shortest verse, but just like the focal verse we are looking at, short but full of meaning and direction.

This "rejoicing" found in Romans 12:15 is both in the present tense and the imperative mode. Previous discussion about these parts of Greek grammar further defines this concept. The rejoicing is to be a lifestyle that is habitual and continuous (present tense) and is seen as a command to us, not just an option for believers (imperative mode). So when we define rejoicing at this point, we must understand that we are talking about a lot of joy and gladness being experienced and expressed on a regular basis. It does seem strange to me that Paul has to command us to be so full of joy, but he does! I am so glad this is so intricately involved in loving one another!

The Description of Rejoicing With One Another

Look very closely at how Paul describes how to rejoice. He uses a particular preposition of great importance, "with." The understanding of this preposition is vital to the description of rejoicing. He tells us to rejoice "with" not "for" one another. It is so amazing to me how one simple preposition could carry such meaning.

Consider the difference between the concepts of "for" and "with." The word "for" indicates external acknowledgement. This has to do with what is emphasized on the outside, acknowledging externally what is happening. It can be perceived in this way, "I am so happy for you." One might be jealous, just putting on a front, or pretending about your situation. When it comes to "with," it's a totally different story.

The preposition "with" carries the meaning of experiential accompaniment, a joining in. This is like playing an instrument in a symphonic orchestra. You are joining in and sharing the joy and excitement of the entire group. Compared to the concept of "for," there is a world of difference. One is standing on the outside looking in while the other is right there on the inside sharing in the joy! In other words, rejoicing with one another can be described as entering in with another's joy and sharing it with them. God so much desires for us to love in this way!

A beautiful illustration of this is found in the story of Luke 15 often referred to as "the prodigal son." The younger of two sons takes his inheritance early and goes off to the big city to essentially waste his life away. Finally when this younger son comes to his senses and returns home penniless and broken, he is surprised to find his father waiting and looking for him. His father comes running to him the moment he sees him. In a wonderful picture of how our Heavenly Father looks and runs to us the moment we start coming to Him, this boy's father in total mercy and forgiveness, restores the boy to his place as his son.

He throws an extreme party for everyone to come and rejoice with him because the son has returned. Everyone seems to be having a great time except for the elder brother. This older son is absolutely put out over the whole thing. He will not even come into the house to enjoy the festivities but stays outside sulking in the dark. The father comes out to him and does everything possible to get the elder son to realize how wonderful of an event this is, but the son refuses. The story ends with the father indicating that it was right to rejoice.

This story reflects many present day congregations. It is a sad commentary on the Christian church today, but is a great illustration of this concept of rejoicing with one another. God doesn't want us standing on the outside missing all the blessings, He desires for us to enter in with others for what He is doing in their lives and share in the joy, to rejoice with them! In all of this the description becomes clear. I would like to give it to you plain and simple in three easy steps:
1. Entering into someone's positive experience.
2. Experiencing the joy of their experience in your heart.
3. Reflecting joy back to them in meaningful words from your heart.

This is a positive participation in one another's lives. This is true fellowship in its fullest actualization. This is not just a concept, it is for real and is effectual for everyone involved in the process.

Consider for a moment the results of what happens in this transaction. As we enter in, experience with, and reflect back the blessing, joy is magnified in the person who first experienced it. It becomes enlarged, it gets bigger. The original joy and blessing someone had now increases in them because you have shared it together. It is magnified in them.

Secondly, the joy is multiplied in that it is now in you as well in them. The joy is not diminished at all but spreads and multiplies, just like the miracle of the loaves and fishes found in the Bible! What is so interesting about this whole process is that it doesn't matter how many people are involved. There is as much joy to share and spread, as there are people willing to enter in and rejoice with one another! Praise the Lord! This is something miraculous!

Now, let's take a second and consider an awesome insight that surfaces here. I believe that most people really think that their greatest source of joy comes from getting something new, a new car, house, furniture, a new job, new friends, or even a new partner. There is joy for sure in these things but the greatest source of joy is in rejoicing with one another! Let me say it like this, the key to a joy-filled life is in rejoicing with one another! This bears repeating for emphasis, the key to a joy-filled life is learning and practicing rejoicing with one another! It might help to make this one of the mantras we say over and over again to ourselves. What is so breathtaking for me is that this is all a part of what it means to love one another. Doesn't God know what He's doing? When He commanded us to love one another, He knew this kind of loving would provide the source for a joy-filled life. Again, this is what everybody is dying to discover. Here it is, let's do it!

The Difficulties of Rejoicing With one Another

It seems so simple, so clear, then why are so few experiencing it? Are Christians just ignorant or are there other matters hindering us? This section will take a brief look at 6 different issues that stand out as difficulties to rejoicing in the way we have described it. I am sure there are other matters I won't mention, but these are primary in my thinking and experience.

The first issue that presents a difficulty for rejoicing with others is the matter of personal woundedness. This is having a broken heart. Proverbs 18:14 says, "The spirit of a man will sustain him in sickness, But who can bear a broken spirit." This verse tells how when the heart of a person is broken, they become dysfunctional in normal activities. There is not one of us alive that hasn't experienced a broken heart because of great or perceived loss. During that time of woundedness, it's very hard to feel joy along with the pain. We are in need of healing. Once we can go through the process of healing, we can enter into another's joy much easier. The caution here to mention is that there are too many Christians stuck in their pain. The woundedness from the past continues and there is no healing desired or has yet been found. We must take a hard look deep inside from time to time to make sure there are no hurts lingering, unresolved. Jesus has promised in Luke chapter 4 that He came to heal the brokenhearted. There is healing available to every believer. It's a part of our salvation.

Another issue that presents difficulties to rejoicing with others is the matter of fear. Fears of all kinds can interfere, disrupt, and block moving into meaningful relationships with others. Proverbs 29:25 says, "The fear of man brings a snare…" Romans 8:15 declares, "For you did not receive the spirit of bondage again to fear…" Paul seems to indicate here that fear and bondage are connected together. Freedom in Christ from our fears allows us to enter in with others to share their lives and particularly their joys. Fear will only bind us and keep us from the potential of this experience.

A third issue presenting difficulties is the matter of selfishness. When we are selfish, there is little interest in the blessings of others. When positive things happen in the lives of others it is more a source of jealousy than joy for the selfish individual. Selfishness keeps us at least at arms length from others. James 4: 1-4 states,

"Where do wars and fights come from among you? Do they not come from your desires for pleasure that war in your members? You lust and do not have. You murder and covet and cannot obtain. You fight and war. Yet you do not have because you do not ask. You ask and do not receive, because you ask amiss, that you may spend it on your pleasures. Adulterers and adulteresses! Do you not know that friendship with the world is enmity with God? Whoever therefore who wants to be a friend of the world makes himself an enemy of God."

These are some strong words! They all have to do with this matter of selfishness and how selfishness will destroy relationships around you. You cannot experience the joy from others when you are in battle with them. We need to lay our selfishness down by crucifying our flesh on a daily basis. As long as there is selfishness on our parts, it will prove to be quite difficult to rejoice with one another.

A fourth issue is bitterness. This has to do with unresolved hurts and offenses in our past that have now turned into bitterness. This

THE FORGOTTEN COMMANDMENT

bitterness is like an emotional cancer eating away at our emotional and spiritual lives. It stands like a huge brick wall keeping us from truly entering into the lives of other Christians. We usually just fake most of our relationships and the others are only superficial. The bitterness inside is hard at work to steal any joy from our lives especially any joy that might come from other believers. Hebrews 12:15 informs us to beware "lest any root of bitterness springing up cause trouble, and by this many become defiled..." Bitterness literally pollutes and defiles everyone around it. The former chapter on forgiveness provides information to the only way to appropriately deal with this matter. It might be good to go back and review it again!

Another issue creating enormous difficulties is jealousy. Jealousy essentially is about discontentment. In one way, jealousy says, "I'm not content with who, what, or where I am." Because of this discontent, when others are blessed and we find out about it, we want it to happen for us. There can be no rejoicing with another when you're upset about being left out of God's blessings. You feel like you're the one that should be getting this stuff not someone else! These feelings and thoughts override any ability to rejoice with someone else. Proverbs 14:30 says, "A sound heart is life to the body, but envy is rottenness to the bones." Proverbs 27:4 also says, " Wrath is cruel and anger a torrent, but who is able to stand before jealousy?" How we need a fresh revelation of who we are in Christ and what God is doing everyday in our lives to combat this wicked spirit.

Some of the greatest achievements of my life were occurring. I came from simple and common roots. My father never finished high school because he had to go to work to help support his family. My mother finally earned her GED when she turned 62 years old. Education and high-level achievement was not a high priority in my family. But I was the first person in my entire extended family of over 200 people to graduate from college with a bachelor's degree. I didn't stop there, I went on to earn my Master's degree. 15 years later, under the encouragement of my wonderful wife, I pursued and earned a Ph.D. in Psychology. While earning the doctorate, I wrote my first book, "Unlocking The Gates of Hell," and developed both these teachings on loving one another and the training on inner healing that is now being used in many places.

In addition, my preaching moved into a new anointing where God's power was released every time I spoke. It was marvelous and supernatural! A colleague close to me that I thought was rejoicing with me over these wonderful accomplishments was only superficially or just plain faking it to my face. There came a time when his jealousy became quite evident and he seemed to lead the charge to demonize my whole life. I was devastated and wanted to retaliate because every accusation was false, but the Lord specifically instructed me to remain completely silent, even if I looked guilty. Obedience towards the Lord was the requirement for me. The Lord would deal with other matters. I was to remain in the place of loving others regardless of what they said or did to me. What could have resulted in tremendous joy for many, turned out to be a bitter experience, because of jealousy. It was very difficult, but I remained faithful to the Lord and His will for my life.

The point of this story is that jealousy can be hidden from view but it ultimately reveals itself sooner or later and it always robs the one who holds it of having any meaningful relationships with others. Jealousy will keep you from rejoicing with one another and from loving one another, no matter how well you think you can fake it. You can't fool God, He sees your heart!

The last issue is pride. This is probably the most dangerous one of all because anyone who has pride is totally unaware of it. Everyone except for you is aware of it. It demonstrates itself in the attitude that you think you know more than anyone else. You can do things better, or you may feel like you're better than most. Pride rises up in your heart to think you're the most important person around and your opinions matter the most. You love to be in charge and to direct others because you feel you're so much better than they, and the list goes on and on. In this elevated state of mind, you cannot enter into other people's worlds or experiences and share their joy. They are down there and you're up here. You are separated from them for whatever justification you have dreamed up and so entering in their life is not even an option. Your only relationship with others is based on how they can serve you and your objectives best. There is nothing else you desire from them.

This matter of pride is what caused the downfall of Lucifer from heaven and ultimately resulted in the sinful fall of all of mankind. Pride is dangerous and deadly to everything that is of God and His purposes. Rejoicing with one another is greatly hindered by pride and only through genuine godly humility can the situation be reversed!

As I stated earlier, there are other issues you might think of that also create difficulties in rejoicing with one another. The important matter is that we face them and deal appropriately with them in order for us to better obey the Great Commandment to love one another.

Rejoicing with one another is a fantastic way of walking in God's blessings and loving others. This activity truly deepens relationships and unleashes the joy of the Lord in all involved. I just love the fact that God has provided the way to live a joy-filled life through practicing this verse and concept. I want to seriously challenge you to begin searching for other believers who are experiencing blessings from the Lord and enter into those blessings with them. You will see the power of this principle and have a great time meanwhile, all the time increasing your ability to love one another to a deeper dimension!

Weeping With One Another

Here are ten words of wisdom I've come to know in life:
1. Don't let your worries get the best of you, remember, Moses started out as a basket case!
2. Some minds are like concrete, thoroughly mixed-up and permanently set!
3. People are funny, they want the front of the bus, the middle of the road, and the back of the church!
4. Many folks want to serve God, but only as advisers!
5. God Himself does not propose to judge a man until he is dead, so why should we?
6. You can tell how big a person is by what it takes to cause him to quit!
7. God promises a safe landing, not a calm passage!
8. When you get to your wit's end, you'll find God lives there!
9. Opportunity may only knock once, but temptation bangs on your door every day!
10. It is easier to preach ten sermons, than it is to live just one!

Living out these one another verses is no easy road to travel. They are tough. I believe I have said this before, if they were easy to do, there would be no need for this book! But just because it takes sincere effort and a lot of the work of the Holy Spirit moving in you, this is no reason to back off or just quit trying. Fulfilling God's Great Commandment is important enough but the benefits of walking these truths out in our lives produce such rich rewards, we are foolish not to put our whole heart in the effort!

Weeping with one another is a good example of how difficult yet so rewarding these truths can be. There are many similarities between weeping and rejoicing with one another. This is why I have put both of these in the same chapter. But please do not overlook the power from these verses to express love to others and to experience how deep and meaningful relationships can occur from living these one another verses.

Again understand that both of these one another verses represent the activities of what loving one another is all about. These truths activated in our lives enhance and liberate relationships to become all that God intends for them to be in our life. Particularly this matter of weeping with one another takes us to the deepest level of relationship possible. Listen to this story I once heard from a servant woman in the Deep South:

A lady in Charleston met this servant who served a neighbor of hers. "I'm sorry to hear of your master-lady's death. You must miss her greatly, you all were such good friends." "Yes mam," said the servant, "I am sorry she died, but we were not friends." "Why," said the lady, "I thought you were. I've seen you laughing and talking together lots of times." "Yes, that's true," came the reply, " We've laughed together and we've talked together often, but we were just acquaintances. You see Ms. Ruth, we ain't never shed any tears together. Folks got to cry together before they become friends." One man said, "The bond of tears is the strongest bond of all."

The Apostle Paul states in Romans 12: 15, "rejoice with those who rejoice and weep with those who weep." Not only are we to rejoice "with" others but also we are to "weep with" others. It is quite interesting to me that the second shortest verse in the Bible illustrates this part of the verse. This verse is found in John 11:35. It simply says, "Jesus wept." Loving others involves deep connections in the emotional dimension. When those we love rejoice, we are able to experience joy with them. When they hurt and suffer, we feel their pain and enter into sorrow with them. The more we love someone, the deeper the connection. This is a painful side of loving others, but it is well worth it from both sides of the fence. We will consider this truth from the same concepts that we examined rejoicing with one another.

The Definition of Weeping With One Another
The Greek word used here for "weeping" literally means to openly show sorrow, to weep out loud. The contrast is with the containing of sorrow within so that no one knows or sees the pain you are in. In other

words, this weeping is about showing sorrow externally and not keeping it a secret or to yourself. Research has demonstrated the destructive effects on the physiological and psychological being by holding negative feelings inside. Learning to express your emotions both positive and negative is very healthy for people. When someone properly 'weeps with" us, the positive outcomes exponentially increase.

When my dad was 80 years old, an aneurysm in his aorta had grown to a dangerous size. If it would burst, he would die within minutes and nothing could be done to save his life. He needed surgery to correct the problem. The needed surgery unfortunately is so serious that older individuals sometimes do not survive the operation. He definitely was at great risk. He did choose to have the operation. I flew up to be with him and to do anything I could to be supportive. The night before surgery and the morning preparation time was difficult for him. He was afraid of the potential of death and actually was convinced he would not survive the day. My father grew up in an era that taught, "men don't cry." He was sincerely suffering inside and kept it all to himself. He was visibly distressed and anxious. I understood some of what he was going through and began to say the right things in order to help him to begin releasing his internal pain and fear. As the tears began to flow, he mentioned the falsehood about men not supposing to cry and I reassured him that was untrue and crying was a manly and healthy thing to do. We wept together there in that isolated room. God showed up, our relationship grew deeper, and peace, strength and courage filled our hearts to face what would come next. He was now in the best emotional condition possible and went through the operation with flying colors. The surgeon told us he was one of his best patients as to how he went through the experience. Do you get the point? Positive outcomes do exponentially increase!

Also in defining this concept of "weeping," consider with me the verbal tense and mode. As with the verb "rejoicing," "weeping" is the same. They are in the present tense and the imperative mode. The present tense indicates the habitual nature of the action. This does not mean that you are to continually go around weeping and demonstrating sorrow. That could be quite depressing for anyone. If we are to rejoice continually also, than that would appear slightly schizophrenic, rejoicing and weeping all at the same time on a regular basis.

Please understand that Paul is trying to emphasize that we are to make these one another verses a lifestyle. When we find someone rejoicing, we rejoice with them. When we discover someone in sorrow, we weep with them. In other words, these activities of love are not to be done only once in awhile in our lives. In building meaningful relationships and loving one another, we practice these concepts whenever needed. This fits directly in the idea of the imperative mode. This is the modality of command. "Weeping with one another" is not an option for the Christian, it is standard equipment. To live the Christian life out by loving one another, we must weep with others. It is a basic requirement of a believer's life.

In summary, weeping is not necessarily shedding tears, although there is nothing wrong with that. "Weeping with one another" involves the open display of sorrow or feeling another person's hurt and pain. In a way you relate and share the pain with them truly feeling it inside of you and expressing it externally with them.

The Description of Weeping With One Another

In the above summary, the description of weeping with one another clearly begins to surface. The consideration of the preposition "with" is crucial for understanding this admonition. It may sound repetitious but it's worth repeating. The idea projected from "with" is an experience of accompaniment rather than an external acknowledgement that is communicated by the preposition "for." It carries the concept of entering into the experience and sharing it with another. This is like playing an instrument in a symphony orchestra. The beautiful music is only created when all instruments are in unison together. "Weeping" with one another is like an emotional song that when it is played correctly produces a meaningful relationship.

In considering this description, there are basically three steps involved. First, there is the entering into someone's negative experience that they share. Second, there is an experiencing of some sense of sorrow within your own heart. Third, out of the sorrow you feel in relationship to the other person's pain, you reflect empathy back to them in brief but meaningful words. It is important to note here that what you reflect back to the person must be very brief, just a sentence or two. The more you say, the more probability of causing a deeper wound to occur in their heart. Later in the practical section, we will discuss this in detail.

Now as this procedure is properly accomplished, consider the results. It is quite amazing what happens, especially in contrast to "rejoicing" with others. When you rejoice with another, the joy is multiplied and increased. In "weeping with another" the opposite occurs. The sorrow in the person is diminished! Pain decreases while joy increases. What a great God we have to provide such powerful and life-giving principles to follow! If sorrow is not shared with another and appropriately dealt with, then the negativity inside the original person is multiplied. This multiplying process of sorrow will transform into horrible emotions and over time demonstrate itself through features such as depression, anxiety, shame, and isolation or what I label disassociation. You can just imagine after a lifetime of unresolved hurts and pain what people live out and become. No wonder there is so much mental and emotional illness in our society! Weeping with one another is the key to mental and emotional health! It also is an important key to building deep relationships!

Now you might share some concern at this point or question this sharing other people's pains and sorrows. Is this Biblical? Is there any foundation or basis in the scriptures for this kind of activity? I'm so glad you asked! Yes there is! The best illustration I can give you is Jesus.

Just consider the life of Jesus and how He related to us. A quick glance at Isaiah chapter 53 will reveal how the Messiah (Jesus) will enter into and experience all of our shortcomings and pains. He did not just sacrifice Himself for our sins, Isaiah informs us in this passage that Jesus entered into our shame, sicknesses, and sorrows to carry them and to become what the writer of Hebrews in 4:15 declares, that Jesus is now our High Priest who can "sympathize with our weaknesses." Notice the concept of "with" here. Jesus has truly experienced all of our pains and hurts as well as our failures. He is able to provide forgiveness, healing, and deliverance because of it. The point here is that He has entered into our negativity in order to help us. We are to continue carrying out His work, this is the good news or gospel we are to live and share with others.

This is also accented in the New Testament by Paul in 2 Corinthians 5:21, "For He made Him who knew no sin to be sin for us, that we might become the righteousness of God in Him." Following in our Lord's footsteps and living out the gospel requires that we demonstrate our love to others by "weeping with" them! This is the best description I can provide. The potential of walking this truth out in our lives carries such potential for our relationships to others and the actual health and well being of all of us. May we see this potential and seek with all of our hearts to give ourselves to relating to others in this way!

The Difficulties of Weeping With One Another

The power of actually operating in this modality in our Christian life is hindered by several major factors. We must face them and do what we can to rid them from our lives. We are all victims of the world around us and are in need of this healing comfort. For too long Christians and churches have experienced weakness and ineffectiveness because of such unresolved hurts within us. There are four specific difficulties I will address here for discussion.

The first difficulty that greatly hinders the ability to "weep with one another" is fear. I have discovered on a number of occasions that people are leery of doing this activity because they are either afraid of not performing it correctly or are afraid of experiencing sorrow altogether. Some feel they have enough pain in their own lives they don't need anymore. It is interesting to point out that when folks begin functioning in this matter that many of their own unresolved griefs are healed. As you become a vessel of the Holy Spirit and His work of comfort through your heart, you often experience the blessing of healing and comfort for your own life. It is remarkable but true. Also, the depth of relationship that this activity leads you into is worth more than gold!

During the time of writing this book, my father-in-law was diagnosed with terminal cancer. Our relationship over 30 plus years never really became very close. Part of the reason is that for most of that time, Brenda and I have been away in the ministry serving the Lord in other states. Our visits were far and in-between. It's hard to develop closeness from a distance. I was blessed to have some time to spend with him in January 2005. During my visits we talked about a lot of matters especially concerning his approaching death. As anyone would be, he expressed deep emotions regarding this. There were some precious times I had with him as I wept with him just like this teaching calls for. The result was an immediate deepening of our relationship. The love we now feel for each other is like a real father and son. I would not take anything for those precious moments together. It is so rewarding when we love one another like God wants us to.

Another difficulty that hinders this action is selfishness. Selfishness by its very nature shows no genuine interest in others. The focal point of attention is self. "My needs" are the most important and only what benefits "me" is worthy of attention. Consideration of another person's pain and suffering is only seen as misfortune but this cannot distract the selfish person from what's really important, and that's "me."

Of course, pride is the third matter on this list. I have already expressed enough information about the destructiveness of pride. Only to say that pride will seek to exclude troubled people from around your life. After all, "I don't want to be affected by all their troubles. I have my image to think about. I need to be rubbing elbows with only the rich and famous or at least with people that are healthy. I don't want to catch what they have." I know, I know, you and I would never say this out loud, but a prideful heart lives out this way. Be careful, pride is very deceitful and tries hard to cover itself up.

The last difficulty worth mentioning is ignorance. This has to do with the fact that we don't know what to say or do so we just do nothing. This may be the greatest barrier of all. Ignorance is no excuse in any situation. Because we are commanded to live in this manner, it behooves us to give considerable attention to learning how to do these activities with excellence. In the next section, we will do just that!

How to Weep With One Another

This particular "how-to" section will be more extensive than the others. This particular "one another" principle is delicate and if you do not perform it correctly, disaster will result. Several individuals through the years have told me that learning how to do this properly has resulted in miraculous occurrences even the rebuilding of several marriages. I cannot over emphasize how vital it is to learn the methodology correctly. Remember that practice makes perfect. Even though at first it may seem mechanical, after you practice for a while, it will become more natural. Primarily, you need to consider the response reflected back to the other person. It would be a good idea to take a look at improper responses first. These are the ones to avoid like the plague!

Unproductive Responses to Hurting People

There are 8 unproductive responses to examine. Some will be more difficult to avoid than others. Please be aware of how sensitive you must be in trying not to use these. There may be a time when some of these might be appropriate but not when comforting or "weeping with" them. I encourage people to only respond in some of these ways when another person specifically is asking for your opinion or advice. Other than a specific request, stay away from them.

1. Logic/Reasoning- This is where you say things such as, " Let me tell you why this happened to you," or, "I think the reason that happened was because...." The person is emotionally hurting. They do not need cognitive stimulation or intellectual ideas, they need emotional comfort.
2. Advise/Instruction- This is where you think the person is ready to put together a better strategy for future planning or something. You might say something like, "Let me give you some things to do to solve the problem," or "Maybe the next time this happens you should ...." Again, at this point, they

are hurting and revealing sensitive pain, they are bleeding. They need an emotional patching not a plan for future reference!

3. Pep Talk- How many of us are guilty of this one! This sounds like, "You're a winner, you'll make it through this. Tomorrow will be a better day." They do not need a pep talk. They need someone to stop the bleeding.

4. Minimize- I witness this often between people. If you want to increase the hurt in someone's life and stop them from ever sharing a hurt with you ever again try this. It sounds like this, "Sure it hurts, but get it into perspective, there's a lot of good going on. Aren't you being over sensitive?" Ouch!

5. Anger- I have to admit, for a long time this was my favorite response to my wife when she shared hurts with me. I did wonder for years why she stopped telling me about any hurts with others, duh! It sounds like this, "That makes me so mad! They shouldn't get away with that! I'm so upset that you keep getting yourself hurt!" Oh yes, this response "really" helps heal wounds!

6. Martyr's Complex- Here is another one of those that causes people to shut down immediately and choose to write you off from their list of friends. It sounds like this, "I had something similar happen to me. I know you feel hurt but after what happened to me, let me tell you what hurt really feels like." This makes someone feel truly comforted and be healed, not!

7. Fear/Anxiety- This is connected to some things previously mentioned. There is a sense that just talking about negative stuff will somehow mysteriously transfer to others. It sounds like this, "I really don't want to talk about stuff like this, it might happen to me too."

8. Spiritualize- This is by far the most common among believers and the most deadly to a hurting individual. Because you use Biblical verses or concepts, this "feels" like the "right" thing to do. After all, using God's word is supposed to help people, right? For the most part this is true, but when you're weeping with another person, attempting to comfort them, this is the worst thing to do! Picture a person just being hit by a car.

There they are, laying in the street, bleeding to death. You run up to them, take a good look and begin quoting scripture and preaching about how God is in control and will take care of all things. Does this help? No! They need first aid, someone to stop the bleeding not to quote Bible passages! This is the same deal. Someone shares openly with you a hurt inside. It may be recent or from their childhood. They finally open up and tell. This is like the scene of the accident described above. Let's comfort and weep with them (stop the bleeding) not get all spiritual with them. As I said earlier, there will be a better time to share teachings from the Word with them.

Productive Responses to Hurting People

Now this is where the rubber hits the road. The accident scene described above is an excellent example of what emotional pain is like inside a person. If they are wounded deeper when they open up and share then the result is usually an emotional shutdown or a building of an emotional fortress to keep others at arms length. When I consider most of the Christians I've known throughout my life, I would characterize them as just this: Individuals behind protective barriers. This is because the church has done such a poor job of understanding and teaching Christians what it really means to love one another. Learning how to do this particular one another verse will absolutely revolutionize your life and others! So, let's discuss how to do it!

First of all, you need to ask the Holy Spirit to make you like Jesus, being filled with compassion. He wants us to be compassionate and to walk like Jesus did among others.

Next, we need to take a moment to look into the person's eyes and try to imagine their hurt and pain. A few seconds of interest into their eyes can reveal much. The eyes are the windows of the soul. As you look into their eyes, you will begin to see and feel some of their pain.

Thirdly, as you speak to them, speak with genuineness from

your heart. You desire to comfort a hurting soul, do it with sincerity. Appropriately use physical touch. Whether it is a touch on their hand or shoulder or a big hug, physical touch communicates warmth and concern.

Next be willing to weep with the person, weeping is a God-given method for releasing internal pain. Even if you're not much of a crying person, you might be surprised at what comes out of you once you emotionally relate with another. Don't force anything. Allow emotions and words to come naturally and sincerely out of your own heart of connecting with their pain.

Finally and most importantly, the less you say the better. The uses of simple statements as provided below are more than adequate. It is the addition of more words that leads you down a trail of moving into unproductive responses. Get over the thought that you have to say something wonderfully intelligent or share revelation from God in order to help. Speaking one simple sentence as the examples below are the most powerful statements anyone could ever say. Afterwards, pray for the person asking God's intervention on their behalf. As you try these you will come to understand what I'm talking about. Remember, one sentence is to be spoken and then just close your mouth! Don't forget this point!

Here are the productive responses:

1. "It deeply saddens my heart that you feel the way you do."
2. "It really hurts me to know that you are hurting."
3. "I am truly sorry you experienced that"
4. "I can see that you are really hurting."
5. "I love you so much. It breaks my heart to see you hurting so much."
6. "I am so sorry you are hurting."
7. Sometimes just to hold a person and cry with them without a word spoken is enough.

THE FORGOTTEN COMMANDMENT

Rejoicing and weeping with one another are vital aspects to loving others. They are the activities of love. Practicing them with others should take place on a regular basis. These can easily be done in the context of a group or in a one-on-one situation. In either of these settings, let one person share a blessing or a hurt in their heart. After they share, each person in the group or the other person (in the one-on-one situation) either practice rejoicing or weeping with them as outlined in the discussion above. Let each person share as appropriate, and then pray for the person who shares. Allow God to pour His Spirit out between you all. I promise, it will be a wonderful experience!

The more we understand what it means to rejoice and weep with others and how to actually carry out these commands, the clearer of an expression of love is visible. In addition, the commandment to love one another is fulfilled more accurately. It seems so simple to me but the Christian world at large has seriously missed the boat on these. It is my prayer and desire that after reading, studying and committing to practice these concepts that your world will be positively affected and real change will occur, both in your life and in the lives of those around you. May God give you the drive and courage to begin to practically living out these truths!

DR. PAUL T. EVANS

Chapter Outline for Preaching or Teaching
(2 Messages)

Loving One Another: Rejoicing With One Another (Rom. 12:15)

Introduction: At times we celebrate our nation's freedom. When it comes to loving others there are 2 elements that when activated enhances and liberates relationships to become all that God intended for them to be.

I. The Definition of Rejoicing with One Another

II. The Description of Rejoicing with One Another

    1. Consider the power and comparison of a preposition:
       (1) "With" – experiential accompaniment
       (2) "For" – external acknowledgement

    2. Consider the description itself:
       (1) Enter into someone's positive experience
       (2) Experience joy in yourself
       (3) Reflect joy back in meaningful words

    3. Consider the result of what happens:
       (1) Joy is magnified in the person
       (2) Joy is multiplied to others

    4. Consider an important insight

III. The Difficulties of Rejoicing with One Another

    1. Personal woundedness
    2. Fear
    3. Selfishness

THE FORGOTTEN COMMANDMENT

4. Bitterness
5. Jealousy
6. Pride

Conclusion: Let's be doers of the word, give it a try!

DR. PAUL T. EVANS

Loving One Another: Weeping With One Another
(Rom. 12:15)

Introduction: Last week we considered the first of 2 elements that when activated enhances and liberates relationships to become all that God intended for them to be in the matter of loving one another.

IV. The Definition of Weeping with One Another

V. The Description of Weeping with One Another

1. Consider the power and comparison of a preposition:
   (1) "With" – experiential accompaniment
   (2) "For" – external acknowledgement

2. Consider the description itself:
   (1) Enter into someone's negative experience
   (2) Experience sorrow in yourself
   (3) Reflect empathy back in meaningful words

3. Consider the result of what happens:
   (1) Sorrow is diminished in the person
   (2) Sorrow is shared with others

4. Consider an important insight

VI. The Difficulties of Rejoicing with One Another

1. Fear
2. Selfishness
3. Pride
4. Ignorance

Conclusion: Let's be doers of the word, give it a try!

Group Study Questions

1. How do you understand what rejoicing with one another means as described in the chapter?

2. How do you understand what weeping with one another means as described in the chapter?

3. How do you see the difference between the two prepositions "for" and "with?"

4. How would you explain how to do each of these one another verses?

5. Explain how doing these verses can build more meaningful relationships with others around you.

6. Why is it so important to say so little when you are weeping with another person?

7. What is the most important thing you learned from the chapter?

CHAPTER SEVEN

Protecting One Another (1Peter 4:8)

The summer of 1959 had come. I was 7 years old, finished the first grade, and confidently felt like a man! Even though I was forbidden to play with matches, their use was no longer a fear, after all fire was something to explore and experiment with (I thought). The woods across from my house looked like an excellent place to begin exploring the nature of fire. I mean, dad and mom just wouldn't understand so I needed a secluded spot to experiment.

Slipping off into the woods early in the morning with a brand new pack of matches in my pocket, I was all set. I found a good spot to begin checking out how interesting fire could be. I do have to say, it felt so mature striking each one and holding it as long as I could. After a few, it got old and I needed to see how fire could consume something more substantial. I gathered a few sticks and leaves and wow, it was so neat to watch those twigs and leaves shrivel up quick as a wink. I was just amazed how fast fire could burn stuff.

It seemed like in the blink of an eye the leaves and sticks surrounding me were catching on fire too. I tried stomping several places to control the situation but before I knew it (you knew this all along, didn't you?), fire was everywhere and growing. Ah my gosh! What to do now? I did what any mature 7 year old would do, I ran like crazy! Approaching the edge of the woods by the street, I carefully looked to see if anyone was around and then darted across the street, into my house, down into the basement and waited. My heart was pounding in my chest especially when 6, I mean 6 big fire trucks arrived on the scene. By now the fire had grown to a 4-alarm blaze and was breath-taking! It took over 8 hours to put the fire out and thank the Lord no one or any houses were harmed!

I was so scared, I didn't know what to do. Of course, everybody in the neighborhood was asking questions. I kept my mouth shut and I figured lying at this point was minor compared to my actions of nearly burning down the neighborhood! When my parents questioned me about the incident, I didn't know a thing!

When I was home visiting at the age of 35, I entered into a discussion with my parents about the fire. I casually mentioned that the authorities never discovered who started that blaze. I confessed to mom and dad that I was the culprit and I was shocked by their answer. They said, "Son, we knew you were the guilty one, but our love desired more to protect you than to expose you to the public humiliation." Wow! They covered my sin!

I know, there are some of you reading this that feel I should have been exposed and face the consequences of my actions. It would have taught me responsibility and I would have learned a great lesson. But you know, I turned out quite responsible without experiencing that. In fact, what I learned that day was more important than anything I might have experienced from public humiliation. I learned that pride will create the environment for destruction and being under proper guidance and supervision will provide the best learning experiences in life. Listen to what the Apostle Peter says in his first epistle chapter 4:8, "And above all things have fervent love for one another, for 'love will cover a multitude of sins.'"

Peter boldly states that real love "covers" other's sins. The Greek word for "cover" means to guard from attack, make provision for, to secure, and to protect. The best way I can define this activity of love is that it is protecting one another. This is just what my parents did for me. The verb is in the present tense that we have come to understand as indicating continual action or a habit. If we are going to love one another then we need to develop a lifestyle where we regularly seek to protect one another!

This one another verse may possibly be the most difficult for you to understand and accept, but in loving one another, it is a must! As hard as it may be to grasp this concept, you must understand that it is essential to apply in relationships. It is crucial to open your heart and mind as we enter into this study because every one of us is in great need to express this as well as to experience this kind of protection from one another.

There are essentially three things we can do when we see or hear something negative about another person. One is to judge the person inside our heart and walk around with that judgment. In chapter three of this book in dealing with receiving one another, we learned that it is God's job to judge and ours to love. This is the case no matter what we see or hear. God is the judge!

Another action is to repeat or tell others about what we have seen or heard. This is called gossip in the Bible and there are many scriptures that clearly condemn this activity. One said, "Well if it's true, it's not gossip." According to the Bible, it doesn't matter if something is true or not. If you tell others who have no power to correct or change something related to a negative matter about someone, than that is ungodly, wicked, and evil gossip. In Proverbs there are multiple verses condemning gossip and in chapter 6:16-19, gossip-like activities are identified as 3 of the 7 abominations to God! So before you choose to say another negative thing remember what you're about to do is seriously disapproved by God.

The third action you can take is to choose to cover and protect the person. Do you know who knows all my sins and shortcomings? My wife and children do but you don't hear a thing about this, why, because they love me. They do not desire public humiliation for me. This is what this verse in Peter and this section is all about. What it really means to love one another is to learn how to protect one another. As we go through this chapter, you will see God's plan and His purpose to multiply real love between Christians in fellowship together and how positive this is for individual believers. We will consider the need for protection, the provision for protection, and the activities of protection. Let's launch ahead!

The Need for Protection

The first thing I want to say is that we all need protection. It can be said that the need is universal. In Romans 3:23, the Bible says, "For all have sinned and come short of the glory of God." Every one of us has fallen short. We have all sinned in one way or another. The truth of the matter is we are continually sinning just about every day. So we all need protection! The Apostle John in 1John 1:8 says, "If we say we have no sin, we deceive ourselves, and the truth is not in us." We are all sinners by nature and there is nothing we can do about that. Believing we can reach a point of perfection on this side of the grave is nothing but a fantasy. It is actually a place of pride, which in itself is a horrible state of sin too! So the glaring truth in all of our faces is that we are all in need of protection.

I have heard some people try to make a case for one sin being worse than another sin. Allow me to let you in on a shocking truth. God sees one sin just as wicked and evil as any other sin. There is no difference to God. They are all bad. Sin is sin to God and we must never forget that. It is man who has attempted to make one sin worse than another in order to serve man's interests or benefits. As you and I can accept this reality, then it's not hard to see where everyone is in need of protection. The need is universal!

Peter in the verse of attention (1 Peter 4:8) also indicates that this need of protection should be a priority in our lives. It is not to be just a casual interest. It is to be in the forefront of our mind and heart. Listen carefully how the verse reads, "And above all things have fervent love for one another...." Did you catch it? "Above all things," means above all things, in plain English, "most importantly!" Peter is not equating this with other matters, he is placing great emphasis on this to be a priority in our love relationships with others. He is strongly declaring that loving one another is the most important thing in the Christian life, which agrees with Jesus' commandment. And the way you demonstrate this love is by covering or protecting others.

Peter uses the imperative mode in the Greek for the verb "cover." This means it is a command not an option. It's not for some Christians to follow but for all. It is a requirement. It is a priority because of the desperate need everyone has for protection!

THE FORGOTTEN COMMANDMENT

Thirdly, Peter indicates that this need of protection is also a stretch for us. It is universal, a priority, and now he explains that it is a stretch. He uses the word "fervent" and states that we are to love one another with this "fervent" love. This Greek word provides the vivid illustration of an athlete stretching every muscle in his body to win a competition. To love fervently is to stretch to the fullest extent possible in order to demonstrate love! There is inherit in this word the concept of intensity and eagerness. This means that loving in this way although it stretches us doesn't necessarily create excessive pain.

As a body builder over many years, I understand the value of extending your muscles beyond the normal range. In fact, for muscular growth to occur, you must stretch them and push them even to the point of discomfort. This is not a negative thing for me at all. It is what I desire because I know the benefits of experiencing this. You may have seen or heard of this saying, "No pain, no gain." There is truth in the statement.

Growing in love will require some discomfort and what I call a stretch. Being in close contact and fellowship with other believers will ultimately result in you seeing or hearing negative things about others. In a family or a family-like group, there will sooner or later be sins revealed, shortcomings, dysfunctions, etc., etc., in each other. It always happens. Normally, responses are judgment, criticism, withdrawal, isolation, and the like. But for those of us serious about loving one another, our response is going to be to protect one another from public humiliation, not just walking away or just plain ignoring matters.

Protecting one another as a form of loving is directly stated in this scripture. To accomplish this effectively, we must first of all have a good understanding that all of us are in need of protection, not just a few. It is obvious that some have a greater need than others and some people's sins are more public than others, but still the fact remains, we all need protection!

The Provision for Protection
Honestly, the question may arise, "Why should I cover or protect my

brother or sister?" Maybe they need public humiliation to teach them a lesson. After all, this kind of behavior has been going on for some time and nothing else has helped, so publicly humiliate them, maybe that will change their lives for the better! This kind of thinking runs rampant in the church among believers. All through history you can find numerous examples of how the church has used public humiliation as a way of trying to correct thousands of other Christians. Unfortunately, there is not one instance from the beginning of time where this methodology has worked. No one ever has changed his life for the better because of public humiliation, not one! But the church continues to walk in utter darkness regarding this issue, continuing to follow this procedure over and over again. Are you receiving any insight into why so many people have left the Christian church or desire no part of it yet?

There is a better way to learn. It would do us good to remember that all of us are sinners and need protection. Consider again the universal nature of the problem. In connection to this, remember the golden rule given by Jesus to us. "Do unto others as you would have them do unto you." If you want to publicly correct others, publicly correct yourself or ask someone else to do it to you, yea, right! I think and hope you get the picture!

I'll tell you how people change. I'll explain what causes individuals to want transformation in their lives... it is loving them like God has loved us! It is applying these principles from this book from scripture that will make all the difference. It is seeking to show your love by protecting others! As I stated before, I know of absolutely no one who has changed for the better by public humiliation. In contrast to that, I have lost count of the number of people I know personally whose lives have not only changed but have been radically transformed by being loved in this way! Oh, that we would crucify our desires to "correct" people by our unloving measures!

Now, lets consider some verses out of Isaiah 53 that provide the basis for this whole discussion.

"Surely He has borne our griefs and carried our sorrows... He was wounded

for our transgressions, He was bruised for our iniquities; The chastisement for our peace was upon Him, and by His stripes we are healed.... And the Lord has laid on Him the iniquity of us all.... Yet it pleased the Lord to bruise Him; He has put Him to grief.... And He bore the sin of many, and made intercession for the transgressors."

It is clear that Jesus paid the price for all our sins. Through His sacrifice, atonement was made for all our errors. Jesus was horribly publicly humiliated for every sin of mankind. Did you catch that? Jesus was publicly humiliated for every one of our sins! If He already took our place and experienced hell and humiliation for us (this is theologically referred to as the substitutionary theory, which all true Christians believe), then please tell me why you or anyone else would think that any person for any sin they've committed, needs to be humiliated again? Because they need correction? Wrong! I already proved this corrects no one! Ah…, ah…, ah, you're on the right track. There is no justification for this behavior towards others!

The only Christian response is to love and cover or protect them! The only one! Any other response is communicating to God that His suffering and sacrifice was not enough. He didn't do a complete job. Now any believer in his right mind wouldn't go there! Protecting one another is about accepting the finished work of Jesus for every one and their sins: past, present, and future. All that is left to do is to love them, love them, and keep on loving them! Excuse me just a second, "Lord, please drive this truth home into the reader's heart right this minute!"

The law of love drives us and demands us to protect our brothers and sisters in Christ! Our job in this whole matter is to release God's love to one another. It is God's job to judge and bring about correction. So, we are to release God's love and let go of any desire or sense of responsibility to judge others. This will ultimately result in major changes in people's lives.

The Resistance to Protection
Even with all of this insight and knowledge, some will continue

not to protect, why? There are some reasons why some find it so difficult to live out loving others by protecting them as described above. There are five particular reasons I would like to mention without too much discussion. I believe for the most part that each one will speak for itself.

1. <u>People are hurting and angry themselves.</u> Striking out and focusing on others seems to bring a kind of sick comfort to their own sense of hurt. In some way focusing on others and bringing pain to them causes them to forget about their own pain for a while. There may be some sense where they are projecting their anger caused from their own hurts to another whereby "punishing " them for their pain. This is obviously sick but very true!

2. <u>A person is just plain malicious.</u> This may be a troubled personality or it might be connected to jealousy or some other reason to be vengeful toward another.

3. <u>Some are just ignorant of what they are doing.</u> No one has ever taught or explained the error of treating other people like this. They have witnessed other examples of this and believe this is standard operating procedure for the Christian life. As far-fetched as this may sound it has been true for a few I've known.

4. <u>Many people have a loose tongue.</u> They just can't seem to keep things to themselves. The sense of feeling like they need to tell someone is like a bubbling cauldron within them. Their need is for healing. The scripture does have a lot to say about a loose tongue. It might be good to do a personal study on this asking the Holy Spirit for assistance if you struggle with this.

5. <u>Some have a low self-esteem.</u> A low self-esteem often demonstrates itself by needing to put others down. By putting other people down you feel like you're at least now their equal or a little above them. Others feel like they're no good so no one else must be good either. We all need to be punished in some way. Again, another sick way of treating others.

No matter what the case, we all need protection and loving one another means protecting. Thank God for His wonderful provision through Jesus Christ that makes it possible to have peace in protecting others. Also I am thankful that in protecting others, the greatest potential for change can occur in their lives!

The Activities of Protection
Now that we have come to this place of understanding the significance of protecting others, lets consider how we do it. There are simply three factors involved in this process. Although the factors are basic and simplistic, their importance cannot be overlooked. Practical application is the goal of this book. So, lets take a look at them.

The first thing to do is to choose to have a real heart's desire to protect others. The volitional part of our being must be exercised. "I choose by the act of my will to begin protecting others." Based on your understanding of how important this is and how this action proclaims the finished work of Jesus, ask God to stir up your heart to desire to want to protect. This is a part of what it really means to love others. So, God help us to have a genuine "want-to."

The second factor in this activity is to forgive. Even though a person's sins do not directly affect us, to protect them you need to enter into the knowledge that Jesus has forgiven them and you choose to join Him in this forgiveness. If you can forgive, you can then protect. This doesn't excuse behavior, it forgives behavior. There is a big difference. In our choice to forgive we also need to choose not to gossip. This means we don't talk about it with anyone. It is laid aside under the blood of Jesus. You are attempting to cover not to expose.

The third factor has to do with dealing with the person about it if you can. If you're hearing trash about another person just refuse to listen and rebuke the person gossiping to you. Tell them to go to the person they're discussing and talk to them not to you. Second-hand information is nothing but gossip. Reject all gossip and redirect the gossiping individual. If you have first hand knowledge, then choose to talk with the person privately ministering to them. Follow the instructions clearly presented in the chapter on forgiveness.

That's it! It is really quite simple. It does take an act of your will to choose to do these and my prayer is that you will. Let's start demonstrating our love to one another by choosing to protect our brothers and sisters today! In fact, like Peter says, "And above all things have fervent love for one another, for love will cover a multitude of sins." I would like to close this chapter with an interesting story from the Old Testament that clearly illustrates this powerful feature of loving one another.

The great flood had subsided. Noah and his family were beginning to repopulate the earth and the world was moving on. Noah had taken an interest in farming and planted a vineyard. After harvesting his crops, he made some wine and unfortunately drank too much. He was so drunk that he lost all sense of his inhibitions and stripped off his clothes. What a spectacle he must have been! Laying drunk and naked, his son Ham saw him and choose to go "outside and tell his two brothers." Essentially, Ham went to gossip about his father's sin outside. He was probably ashamed by his father's behavior. How could he do that being Noah and all, but he did. The other two sons of Noah after hearing about the situation made quite a different choice. They came to their father with a blanket in their hands, wouldn't even look on his nakedness and walked backwards to their father and covered him up. The Bible says, they "covered his nakedness." They covered his sin. They wanted to protect their father. Was Noah guilty? Yes! Did he deserve public humiliation? No! This was love in action!

The story ends with Noah waking up the next day and discovering what his three sons had done. Ham was cursed and the other two sons were blessed! Do you understand? Protecting others will result in blessing, the other activity will bring a curse. What do you want in your life? By God's grace, may we learn to protect one another!

Chapter Outline for Preaching or Teaching

Protecting One Another 1 Peter 4:8

Introduction: When you see or hear something negative about another, you are faced with 2 choices, keep it to yourself or share it with others, which we call gossip. The Bible does have a few things to say about this matter as it is related to loving one another!

I. **The Need for Protection**
   1. It is universal

   2. It is a priority

   3. It is a stretch

II. **The Provision for Protection**
   1. Lets consider Isaiah 53 and the work of Jesus

   2. What are some reasons why people do not protect?
      (1) Hurt and anger
      (2) Malicious
      (3) Ignorance
      (4) Loose tongue
      (5) Low self esteem

   3. Our job in this is to release God's love through our heart.

III. **The Activities of Protection**
   1. Choosing to have a real heart's desire to protect.

   2. Choosing to forgive and not to gossip.

   3. Choosing to help a person if possible ministering to them.

Conclusion: Consider Noah and his sons. If Jesus is real in our life, let's commit to allowing Him to express His love and reality through our lives especially through our tongues!!

Group Study Questions

1. Explain how you understand the universal need for protection.

2. Why do you think protecting one another is such a priority for every Christian?

3. Discuss how you understand Christ's provision for being the basis of protecting one another.

4. What are some reasons you can think of why believers don't always protect one another?

5. How do you understand God's job and our job in all of this?

6. How does the story of Noah and his sons impact you?

7. What is the most important thing you received from this chapter?

CHAPTER EIGHT

Bearing One Another Burdens (Galatians 6:1-5)

Frightening is one way of describing the time in the lives of most Central Floridians in the summer of 2004. Several hurricanes arrived on our shores that devastated both coastlines across the interior of Central Florida. Living in Melbourne, Florida, I experienced the devastating north eye of two of the storms. I can say first hand that it was quite scary. The aftermath of the storms and clean up was taxing to say the least. Traveling around and finding necessary supplies because of the loss of utilities was at times an all day task. Lives of many people were totally altered in those few short weeks.

But the actions on the part of so many demonstrated the caring and love for the hurting. Untold stories of sacrifice and giving were the normal activity of those days. It was exciting to me to hear and see such devoted acts of love from so many people. Spontaneous acts of generosity occurred everywhere! After one storm, the American Red Cross distributed 400,000 meals in less than one week. In North Port, in the parking lot of the South Biscayne Baptist Church, volunteers with the Southern Baptist National Relief Team began cooking at 4a.m. every morning. There were over 200 men from the same organization camped out in the First Baptist Church of Melbourne, going out everyday to assist in cleaning up and repairing whatever they could. Christians and non-Christians from far and wide came to help bear the burden of our trouble. What a wonderful sight!

I would like to say this is the norm for the human race but it's not. It usually takes a major disaster like a hurricane or a tsunami to bring out this kind of concern. It is the Lord's desire that believers learn how to bear one another's burdens as a lifestyle rather than just in the time of dire emergency. Bearing one another's burdens is what I call the completion of what it means to love one another. In the passage of focus, the Apostle Paul lays out a clear teaching and direction to follow in living this principle out in our lives.

Living in this world is almost a guarantee that sooner or later, you will be faced with very difficult burdens. Many burdens are nearly unbearable and can interrupt, detour, or even destroy a person's well-being or life in general. I have some wonderful news that God has a plan of how you can live victoriously even in light of the reality of life-threatening burdens! Also, as we consider what it really means to love one another, learning to bear one another's burdens will produce deep connections of relationships with others. In addition, the complete picture of what it truly means to love one another will be displayed. There is some confusion in Christian circles as to what bearing burdens actually means. Paul provides the information we need to know in appropriately bearing one another's burdens in this passage, so let's dive in!

Clarifying Burdens

The first area I want to discuss is in clarifying "burdens" because there seems to be a contradiction in the passage. We are told to "bear one another's burdens and then we are directed to "carry our own burdens." Which is it? Let's make up our mind here. A close examination of the Greek reveals the clarity and meaning for understanding.

The first "burden" is the Greek word, "baros." This is the burden others have that we are to carry or assist with. This word means a load to heavy to carry alone. This word carries with it the idea that the load is so heavy that to attempt to carry it alone would result in injury. I have interviewed and counseled with numerous individuals through the years that have tried to carry these kinds of burdens alone. Emotionally, spiritually, and even their physical bodies have suffered injury resulting in the need for professional help. Some have suffered what appears to be irreversible damage to their personality. Apart from a Divine miracle of healing, they will never be whole again. When we have a "baros" type burden, we need someone to help us to bear or carry it with us! These are the kind of burdens Paul directs us to bear with others. This is the completion of loving one another.

The second "burden" is the Greek word, "phortion." This is the kind of burden Paul tells us that we are to carry for our self. This Greek word is the word for a backpack or a soldier's kit. This is a load one is expected to carry alone. This kind of backpack normally includes the essential items needed for a journey. Paul is indicating in the passage that this "phortion" type of burden is a backpack full of the necessary Christian disciplines needed for Christian living. To expect another to "carry" you through your Christian life is ridiculous. We are expected to grow-up and reach for maturity in our own Christian life.

The Three Sources of Burdens

Now, in understanding that we are talking about "baros" type of burdens, Let's move on. There are three sources of burdens that require help in carrying. One of those sources is the consequence of sin. It is true that forgiveness is an immediate commodity obtained from the Lord, but please understand that forgiveness is not an escape from the consequences of sin. Forgiveness doesn't eliminate the natural outcomes from living a sinful life or even committing one sin.

If you violate your body by using alcohol, drugs, and smoking, than more or less you will suffer the results of long-term usage. Lung cancer should not be a surprise for someone who has smoked for twenty years. Losing a family, resources, or ending up in jail should not be a shocking reality to someone using alcohol and drugs. The physical and psychological damage that occurs through sinful lifestyles is not immediately reversed just because forgiveness is experienced.

If you rob or murder another person for any reason, you will probably end up in prison and maybe for a long time, even if was the first time you ever committed a crime. You can be forgiven immediately, but the consequences continue. This is not a hard concept to conceive. But, regardless of the reasons of the consequences, the burden left to bear is more than one can carry without help. Carrying the burden of the consequences alone only results in personal injury. This is not God's plan even though we brought it upon ourselves. God's plan is for someone to love us and to help carry the burden.

Another source of burdens comes from the adverse circumstances of life. The Bible indicates that it "rains on the just and unjust alike." We live in a fallen world. This means that all of creation is affected negatively by the fall of mankind in sin and no person regardless of belief is exempt from some of these adverse circumstances. Cancer and other serious illnesses happen to good and godly people no matter how strong their faith is. Accidents and injuries can occur to the best people you know. Financial disasters along with difficult losses of all kinds are just around the corner for anyone. We would be foolish to think that believing in Jesus Christ creates immunity from all of this. This is a cheap version of the gospel not found in the scriptures! The potential for adverse circumstances to occur in our lives is real. When they happen, we need others to shoulder the burden with us to help.

A wonderful friend of mine was experiencing the Christian community we built around these teachings. His life as well as mine grew in Christ and deepened in the loving environment of these "one another verses." I watched him change from an emotionally closed individual to an outgoing, giving, openly loving person. Everyone around him was affected by his change. The beauty of the Lord that had always been in him was in full blossom.

The news that came next was unbelievable; his body was filled with cancer! With each visit and procedure, the news got worse. He had cancer all through his body and there was nothing man could do. Over the next few short months, he put up the biggest fight I have ever seen a man give to cancer. His faith enlarged and everyone with him believed a miracle was on the way. He spent hours on end examining his life to ensure all was right in God's eyes. He did not want anything to hinder the supernatural work of the Lord in his life. But the inevitable happened, he died. The burden was more then we could bear alone. It was the loving expression of a community of believers who understood how to bear one another's burdens that eased the sheer horror of losing such a good husband, father, and friend.

Life in this world is fragile. There is a guarantee of breakage some where along the way. God has provided the way to help in the bearing and healing of those times, "bearing one another's burdens."

The third source of burdens comes directly from activity from the enemy of our souls. Peter informs us that the devil is roaming around looking for anyone to take advantage of and destroy. Paul instructs us in Ephesians chapter 6, that we are in a hand-to-hand combat situation with the devil not with the things we are able to see. The truth of the matter is that the devil hates us and will stop at nothing to shame, blame, and destroy us! He knows that his time is limited and is actually running out of time, so his efforts against us will increase. Peter tells us that we are not to think it is strange when all manner of "fiery trials" come upon us. The work of the enemy will at times be a great burden, a "baros" burden to us.

Although we are to expect this, don't be fooled into thinking that you can face these times alone! God never tells us to walk through these by ourselves. The whole purpose of Paul's admonition to bear one another's burdens is about doing just that! The Lord understands how difficult these burdens are to us, that's why He provides such clear direction to believers in knowing how to help one another. In fact, this is all a part of the plan of God in what it means to love one another!

An Important Insight

It is very important to understand that bearing one another's burdens does not mean that the burden disappears or full healing is released for someone. Bearing the burden simply means that we are carrying the burden with another person. I do have to say that all "baros" burdens are intended for sharing and without this sharing including the subsequent bearing of a burden, they will never be effectively dealt with!

Some burdens will be diminished in time. Others will need special attention like counseling, inner healing, and other helps of this nature. Still others will need divine intervention in order to be removed. But in any case, burdens must be shared (someone bearing the burden with you) to begin the process.

Consideration of the Meaning of Bearing

Let's turn our attention to the Greek word Paul uses for "bearing."

The word means to carry, uphold, support, or to bear. There can both be an external as well as an internal significance to this word. An example would be like when Jesus carried the cross (externally), He was also carrying our sins (internally). In other words, "bearing" can mean something we do visibly and outwardly or it may be something deep in our heart or both.

The caution to mention here is that this is not an excuse for enabling or taking responsibility for another person. This is about supporting them in a burden, not taking it from them. There is a world of difference between the two.

There are always some who would like you to take all responsibility for their lives. Every problem they face, they desire someone to fix the problems and care for them. This is not the case at all when it comes to "bearing one another's burdens." The words best describing "bearing" are support and help, not fix and solve. But the image of being in the difficulty with another person is there.

"Backdraft," a motion picture about fire fighters was quite popular several years ago. The particular company of firemen highlighted in the film were very committed together. In one scene, one fireman had fallen through the floor and was about to fall into a raging fire. Another fireman had a hold of his arm doing his best to keep him from going into the fire. They were both slipping and the falling man said, "Just let me go!" Just then, several others arrived on the scene and all jumped to the rescue. The original man holding on to his arm cried out, "If you go, we all go!" This is the perfect illustration of "bearing one another's burdens."

What an attitude to have in the church among Christians! If only our love for one another was of that caliber so that as one falls under a burden, others would come along side sharing the burden to say, "If you go, we all will go with you!" This is the kind of church the world is looking for!

Another important feature to consider about this word "bearing" is the Greek grammar. As with other verbs we have examined, this word also is in the present tense and the imperative mode. The present tense speaks to the habitual activity of the action directing it to become a lifestyle. The imperative modality indicates the command to do it. This action of "bearing" is essential in following Christ and fulfilling His command to love. It fits into place as another piece of the puzzle of the complete picture of what it means to love one another!

The Results of Bearing One Another's Burdens

The results we discover are simple and clear. There are actually two basic outcomes. First, bearing one another's burdens lightens the burden and lessens the injury. After all, this was the original purpose. The "baros" burden is too heavy to carry without personal injury. No matter what the source of the burden or how responsible we are for the burden, God loves us so much, He desires for another believer to bear it with us.

The second result is spelled out clearly in the text itself, "and so fulfill the law of Christ." Bearing one another's burdens is so powerful that it completes the "law of Christ" which is love! Discussing the matter of loving one another finds it's completion in learning how to bear one another's burdens. Praise the Lord! Is there someone you know who has fallen, is falling, or will fall through the floor soon? The fire is waiting to devour them. Will you be ready and willing to run to their rescue, hold on tight and say, "If you go, we go!" May God speak to our hearts of the utter necessity of living out our Christian lives in this fashion and not allow any imitation to take its place!

A Practical Suggestion

I don't think it's a good idea to run out looking for burning buildings yet! But there is something you can do right now in your group together or if you might want to do this individually with someone. Allow a person to share a genuine burden in their life. Practice the technique you learned in the chapter on "weeping with one another" with the person first.

Second, inform the person sharing that you would like to bear that burden with them and give them a piece of yarn (any color will do just fine) about eight inches long. Let them tie it securely around your wrist. Trim it up with scissors. Let them know you will be thinking and praying for them every time you see or feel this around your wrist. Only let it come off when it wears out. Bathe in it, play in it, etc., etc. As God brings thoughts and ideas into your mind during this time, contact them to let them know you're praying or whatever else God directs you to do. I think you have the idea, try it!

A fringe benefit of this "burden bracelet" is that somebody will probably ask you what is that for and you can share with him or her. It's a great witnessing tool and lets others know you're serious about praying for others. When they need real prayer, I wonder who they will seek out?

Chapter Outline for Preaching or Teaching

Bearing One Another's Burdens (Gal. 6:1-5)

Introduction: Living in this world is almost a guarantee that sooner or later, you will be faced with very difficult burdens. What are we to do to maintain our joy and peace with the Lord?

I. Clarifying "Burdens"
   1. Examining 2 words in scripture
      (1) "Baros" –
      (2) "Phortion" –

   2. Considering 3 sources of burdens
      (1) Consequences of sin.
      (2) Adverse circumstances of life.
      (3) Oppression from the enemy.

   3. 3 ways burdens can be removed
      (1) Some will be diminished naturally in time.
      (2) Some will take effort on our part.
      (3) Some will need divine intervention to be removed.
   4. 1 general principle: In any situation, burdens must be shared in order to effectively deal with them.

II. Defining "Bearing"
   1. The meaning of the word –

   2. The verbal action of the word –

   3. The results of practicing this:
      (1) It lightens the burden of another.
      (2) This is so powerful that it fulfills the law of Christ!

Conclusion: Let's begin bearing one another's burdens!

Group Study Questions

1. Explain how the two words for burden in Galatians are different.

2. What are the three sources of where burdens come from?

3. Why do you believe God wants us to bear these burdens in others even if they are solely responsible for them?

4. What does the meaning of the word "bearing" mean to you?

5. How do you understand that by bearing one another's burdens you fulfill the law of Christ?

6. Share an experience of what it felt like when someone helped carry one of your burdens or what you think it would feel like for someone to do this for you.

7. What was the most important thing you learned from this chapter?

CONCLUSION

So there you have it! This is what it really means to love one another. I believe Jesus communicates clearly through His own words and actions recorded in the New Testament along with His immediate followers that the most important command to follow in the Bible is to love one another! Scripture after scripture, story after story, the entire message of Christ is about this world-changing love. This love began in the heart of God, was demonstrated through the life of Jesus, and now is to continue through believers empowered and full of the Holy Spirit! Genuine success in the Christian life is measured by God's standard who looks on our hearts seeking obedience to this command. I believe the reason why so many Christians and churches are struggling is because they have forgotten this commandment. It's time to rediscover it and with all of our hearts seek to employ it in our lives!

In our time together we discussed the 7-fold understanding of loving one another. Greeting one another is the beginning of love. Being kind to one another is the over-arching attitude of love. Receiving one another is the basic foundation of love. Forgiving one another is the main ingredient of love. Rejoicing and weeping with one another are the activities of love. Protecting one another is the full extent of love. Finally, bearing one another's burdens is the completion of love. Every one of these verbs is in the present tense and the imperative mode. In other words, a commanded lifestyle of Christianity! So what are we waiting for?

Without love we are nothing according to the Apostle Paul in 1 Corinthians 13. I don't know about you, but I'm committing myself to this kind of loving one another for the rest of my life! It may not build fancy buildings or develop breath-taking programs for thousands of spectators to awe of, but it will provide the depth, meaning and realness to the kind of life I'm searching for here on earth and looking forward to in heaven! Will you join me right now, and let's touch first base!